*For Car
wit*

D1086344

/86

A Celebration for Stanley Kunitz

A Celebration for Stanley Kunitz

On His Eightieth Birthday

The Sheep Meadow Press
Riverdale-on-Hudson, New York

© 1986 by The Sheep Meadow Press. All rights reserved.
Published 1986

Printed in the United States of America

The Sheep Meadow Press, Riverdale-on-Hudson, NY
Distributed by Persea Books
225 Lafayette St., New York, NY 10012

A Celebration for Stanley Kunitz

Library of Congress Preassigned Catalog Card Number:

86-060942

ISBN 0-935296-60-X (Paper)

Typesetting by Keystrokes, Lenox, Mass.
Cover design by Wongi Sul

Portrait of Stanley Kunitz, by Philip Guston
Charcoal drawing, 1959

Contents

A Celebration for Stanley Kunitz

Marie Howe

A Letter to the Editor

Dear S.,

...Certainly every poem I've written has Stanley's breath in it. By that I mean that in a real sense he is standing over my shoulder as I write, and more importantly, re-write. He reminds me to let the image do the work, to cut out the exposition so that the reader will have something to do other than go "hmmm." Many times I have stomped back and forth over his carpet arguing over a word or a stanza to see, after a few days, if not a few minutes, with a sudden shocking clarity, that he was right. I have never known anyone who can so perfectly see the underbelly of a poem, the inner construction on which it hangs.

Conjuring Stanley makes me braver, gives me the heart to go deeper. Not only is he a great poet, but also a great and luminous man. *You* know all this, but his love of the world, the rocks and flowers and animals, the bleeding breathing stuff of it, is as inspiring to me as the poems he writes. Stanley has managed to do what many of us fear is impossible. He is a poet and he is sane. He is *of* this world and from there he speaks. And he shines even as he turns into dark and deeper dark. When I write, it is his courage and his luminosity that I conjure as much as his poems, which seem born from both rock and water.

The miracle of his teaching is that he influences me to be myself, not him, or anyone else. He encourages all his students to have the muscle and heart to write their own stories. In that way, he profoundly changed my life, and for that insight and generosity I can never thank him enough.

I include both published and unpublished poems, and leave the choice, if there is one, to your discretion. But finally, thank you for doing this. It is a great and good thing. Another miracle Stanley has made happen is that there is, among his tribe of friends and students, a kind of

3

communion that is our common love for him. Whenever I meet someone who also loves Stanley, my heart instantly opens. Many others have mentioned this, and in this way his heartfelt gesture multiplies, connecting and reconnecting. What better gift for his 80th birthday than to show him this, to give him back his own garden, all blooming and fluttering in his hand?

If I am fortunate enough to be included in such a gift, I will be deeply happy. In any case, it gives me great joy to know it's going to happen for him.

Marie

Mary Oliver

Stanley Kunitz

I used to imagine him
coming from the house, like Merlin
strolling with important gestures
through the garden
where everything grows so thickly,
where birds sing, little snakes lie
on the boughs, thinking of nothing
but their own good lives,
where petals float upward,
their colors exploding,
and trees open their moist
pages of thunder—
it has happened every summer for years.

But now I know more
about the great wheel of growth,
and decay, and rebirth,
and know my vision for a falsehood.
Now I see him coming from the house—
I see him on his knees,
cutting away the diseased, the superfluous,
coaxing the new,
knowing that the hour of fulfillment
is buried in years of patience—
yet willing to labor like that
on the mortal wheel.

Oh, what good it does the heart
to know it isn't magic!
Like the human child I am
I rush to imitate—
I watch him as he bends
among the leaves and vines

to hook some weed or other;
even when I do not see him,
I think of him there
raking and trimming, stirring up
those sheets of fire
between the smothering weights of earth,
the wild and shapeless air.

Christopher Busa

Stanley Kunitz: A Poet in His Garden

"How does a poet garden?" I asked Stanley Kunitz, the lifelong gardener. At 80, he remains vigorous, claiming to have subdued ("through willpower") the arthritis in his lower back. He gardens every summer day at his Cape Cod house, within view of Long Point Light, the beacon at the very end of the spiraling Cape. Here the atmosphere is fabled for its clarity. The light, refracted off the water, has attracted artists since the beginning of the century, when they discovered its power to intensify color. Blues are bluer and greens are greener. Kunitz, a gardener naturally alert to fragrance, notices that this air is "brine-spiked."

Kunitz does most of his writing at night, occasionally working until dawn. His study seems buried in the bottom of the house, a basement cell, spare and tidy and sometimes damp. There is one window; three heaps of compost are the only thing in its view. Beneath the window, out of view, is a narrow area for propagating cuttings. "Imagination," Kunitz says, "implies a surplus energy beyond what is needed for simple survival. When I come to the desk and the poetry, it's after I've used my body up in the day. Then I can move into that interior realm, which is still intact. Working in the garden, I'm always thinking, but often I feel my mind free-floating. I'm concentrating on what I am doing, but there is another level, another tier of the self that is whole and moving in its own secret way."

Although Kunitz lives the greater part of the year in New York City, his favorite writing season is the autumn he spends on the Lower Cape, as his garden is dying out. It is this garden he describes in a recent poem, "The Snakes of September":

> All summer I heard them
> rustling in the shrubbery
> outracing me from tier
> to tier in my garden,

a whisper among the viburnums,
a signal flashed from the hedgerow,
a shadow pulsing
in the barberry thicket.
Now that the nights are chill
and the annuals spent
I should have thought them gone,
in a torpor of blood
slipped to the nether world
before the sickle frost.
Not so. In the deceptive balm
of noon, as if defiant of the curse
that spoiled another garden,
these two appear on show
through a narrow slit
in the dense green brocade
of a north-country spruce,
dangling head-down, entwined
in a brazen love-knot.
I put out my hand and stroke
the fine, dry grit of their skins.
After all,
we are partners in this land,
co-signers of a covenant.
At my touch the wild
braid of creation
trembles.

The "north-country" spruce that figures in this poem is one of four Alberta spruces, roughly placed in the corners of the rectangular garden. They provide an unobtrusive axis that is for the garden's design what a line of association is for a poet: something usually not noticed until it is pointed to. These treelike shrubs are quiet presences a little taller than a man, in the shape of a cone. They seem manicured with a military ceremony, the very embodiment of social order, like a Swiss guard. ("You think they are male?" Kunitz enlightens me, "You have not seen them at dusk, when they are female.")

The most important organizational feature of the garden is a series of terraces that squiggle longitudinally from the street sidewalk to the house. These terraces (the "tiers" in the poem) are built from low brick walls, the serpentine curve of each terrace echoing another as they rise up the very definite slope of the garden. Of course, the brick structure is always half-hidden while the garden blooms—the immediate impression is one of cresting energy, like a giant wave rolling through a beam of sunlight, folding color within color. There are five terraces of varying width, each with drifts of their own colors, whose moments of display are staggered through the season. The central terrace is exclusively blue or blue-purple flowers. Among them: *Veronica, Statice, Salvia, Stokesia, Lisianthus, Campanula, Platycodon, Aster × frikartii.* Kunitz is enchanted by blue, "the most difficult of all garden colors," he says.

He notices the color deepen while the afternoon deepens, "blue-fair and serene," in the words of one poem about Indian summer, which Kunitz also associates with blue. "Yes," he agrees, "blue is a religious color, the color of the spiritual life. I use it as a color stress, for the contrast it provides to the prevailing yellows, pinks and reds, the most common of garden colors."

Kunitz bought this house almost thirty years ago, when the front yard was something less than a garden—it was a barren sand dune. A few wisps of witch grass, but nothing more, grew. The whole area—about 2000 square feet—was unstable. Later, Kunitz would build the soil using his formula for perfection: one-third sand, one-third peat moss, one-third compost, plus plenty of seaweed and cord grass collected off the seabottom at low tide. But first he realized that the only solution for the steep grade of sand was to terrace it. "Then everything fell into place: The garden became like a poem in stanzas. Each terrace is a stanza, or perhaps a section of a poem." Poems are the productions of artists, not engineers, so it is only to be expected that Kunitz, who labored for two summers to prepare his space, struggled like a lord of creation with Formless Matter: "Have you ever worked with live, dry, loose sand?" he asks. "It's like shoveling water."

Over the years his garden has grown elaborate. Each terrace is edged with *Heuchera sanguinea, Dianthus, Astilbe, Lobelia, Potentilla* or *Ajuga*. I walked on a meandering pine-bark path over the crest, past *Hibiscus syriacus* 'Blue bird', the cluster of fragrant roses, the variegated hydrangea, past the *Cotinus coggygria* (purple smoke bush) that glows uncannily in the suppressed light of twilight and brushes an adjacent late-blooming Indian-spice *(Vitex agnus-castus)*. Then around the corner of one of the "north-country" spruces, down past the *Euonymus* hedge that shields the garden from the street, arriving now at the front gate where a visitor would enter, taking the flower-lined walk across worn railroad ties to arrive at the front porch, where I would begin again the walk just completed. One could circle endlessly and see new things each time. The height of shrubs and flowers is varied, designed to obscure one view while it reveals another: "a Japanese idea of never being able to see the whole at once," says Kunitz.

A lyric poet is concerned with ways to concentrate experience within a small space. Thus, when Kunitz speaks about the art of poetry he speaks also about the esthetic of his garden: "The work of the imagination is not only in achieving magnification of experience by enlarging it, but also in achieving intensification of experience by reducing it in scale, so it becomes almost like a microscopic field." Because Kunitz's garden is small, every inch of space is used. No part can look bare or unkempt. "Keats's desire to 'load every rift with ore' comes to mind," he says. "I even move plants when they stop contributing. Often I pot them and replace

10

them with others. Later, I replant them. But temporarily they've lost their rental space."

Kunitz inherited one scarecrow of a tree, a chokecherry that was afflicted with numerous ills. It was the only tree on his property. It stood pathetically in a low depression just beyond the boundary of the garden. He recalls, "The tree was ugly. It attracted bugs. It blocked my view." He wanted to chop it down, but did not want the stump. He recalled Martha Graham admonishing her students at Bennington, where Kunitz also taught: "Self-consciousness is ugly!" The sad gesture in the scrawny, gnarled trunk suggested a Graham dance, "The Lamentation."

What to do with the tree? Kunitz says, "I thought I would transform it into something I loved." Somewhat astonished at the confident way he can sound cruel, he explains how he choked the chokecherry by training Baltic ivy to sheath it. He had pruned the branches. The gesture evolved into "an oxymoron," says Kunitz, "both an artifact and something organic." He calls the tree his "Lamentation Tree."

It is the first thing he looks at each morning, he says. The tree is charismatic because it embodies death. "Like us," says Kunitz, "it lives and dies at once." It enacts with upraised, amputated arms the image of the suffering it undergoes. This is a pervasive theme in Kunitz's poetry. A beached whale dying on the beach is magnificent when his parched skin becomes parchment for teenagers to carve their initials on: The whale becomes "like us,/disgraced and mortal."

Searching Kunitz's poetry, I have found a song that his Lamentation Tree sings. It is called "An Old Cracked Tune":

My name is Solomon Levi,
the desert is my home,
my mother's breast was thorny,
and father I had none.

The sands whispered, *Be separate,*
the stones taught me, *Be hard.*
I dance, for the joy of surviving,
on the edge of the road.

Gardening is an aspect of Kunitz's meditative life. "Many
of my poems come to me while I'm working in the garden.
And I feel a direct flow of energy from the earth itself.
When I garden, I'm deep in physical sensations and
nourished by a storm of images. I need these day-by-day
satisfactions."

The poet's garden occupies a semi-public space. A
glimpse is available from the street. The garden itself bor-
rows a view of the bay, across the street. In this bay—Prov-
incetown Harbor—the Pilgrims signed the Mayflower Com-
pact upon their arrival in the New World. (To simplify
history, one might say the Pilgrims left Provincetown and
settled in Plymouth because the soil in Provincetown was
so poor, so sandy, so like the desert of Solomon Levi.) Today,
Provincetown is gregarious, but not Puritan. More like a
Mediterranean fishing village, with the eave of one house
tucked under the wing of another, the town is closely packed
and gets along as an extended family. Portuguese emigrants
from the Azores work a large fleet of fishing vessels, painted
festively in places where the paint is not worn to bare wood.

Another local, democratizing influence is the swelling
population of artists and writers who have colonized the
town. (Notable are Robert Motherwell and Norman Mailer.)
"Is the essence of a private garden privacy?" Kunitz answers,
"My garden is shaped by circumstances. Sure, it's a highly
personal garden, but it's public space. I do control it. The
hedge obliges people to observe the garden from the
wrought-iron gate. I control their angle of vision. I have
thought about shutting off the garden from public view
with a more solid barrier at the entrance. No doubt that
would make me happier; it would also make me guilty. I
am part of this community. To a degree I enjoy sharing it.

People stop and go 'Ooh' and 'Ah' and I say 'Thank you, thank you,' but I do not talk. I often tell them I am the hired hand.'"

Like poetry, gardening can be a technique for enlarging the ego through modesty. "A tendency more and more apparent in modern life is for the artist to cease to be common, to share general concerns. Now he is becoming a specialist, or a technician at an advanced level, really a machine for converting the life into poetry or fiction or painting. One is thinking, 'How am I going to make a little poem out of my knowledge of flowers?' I reject that attitude." Kunitz believes that too many artists today have a tendency to distance themselves from ordinary experience, such as cooking, eating, gardening. "When I was a child growing up in Worcester, Massachusetts, where the woods had spongy paths and were still Indian-haunted, I had a little garden. This, because I wanted to. Nobody told me, do this, do that. I called my first garden a Victory Garden, though I was not old enough yet to know what that meant. I just thought if anything grew, it was a victory."

How does a poet garden? Mostly by caring. "Gardening for me is a passionate effort to organize a little corner of the earth, which I want to redeem. The wish is to achieve control over your little plot so that it appears beautiful, distinguished—an equivalent of your signature in the natural world."

Richard Wilbur

The Rule

The oil for extreme unction must be blessed
On Maundy Thursday, so the rule has ruled,
And by the bishop of the diocese.
Does that revolt you? If so, you are free
To squat beneath the deadly manchineel,
That tree of caustic drops and fierce aspersion,
And fancy that you have escaped from mercy.
Things must be done in one way or another.

Alan Dugan

On Flowers, On Negative Evolution

When the front-end loader ran over my wife's Montauk daisies
I wanted to tell the driver, Butch,—a nice kid—but couldn't:
"No flowers, no us. Flowers are basic to human life.
That's why we think they're beautiful. No flowers, no seeds;
no seeds, no greenery; no greenery, no oxygen: we
couldn't even breathe without them. Also: no greens,
no grasses; no grasses, no herbivorous animals;
no animals, no beefsteaks. There wouldn't be anything
to eat except fish, and no way to breathe unless
we went back to the ocean and redeveloped gills.
There the sea-weeds would make oxygen by flowering underwater,
the way it used to be in the old days, and you
would be running over them in your submarine. This is why
flowers are thought beautiful, and this is why it's important
not to destroy too many of them carelessly, and why you could
have been more careful with my wife's god-damned daisies."

Stanley Moss

Song for Stanley Kunitz

Creature to creature,
two years before we met
I remember I passed his table
at the Cedar Tavern.
He who never knew his father
seemed to view all strangers
as his father's good ghost,
any passing horse as capable
of being Pegasus, or pissing
in the street.
I who knew my father
was wary of any tame raccoon
with claws and real teeth.

At our first meeting 26 years ago,
before the age of discovery,
I argued through the night,
against the tragic sense of life,
I must have thought God wrote in spit.

I keep a petrified clam, his gift, on my desk.
How many times have I kissed the stone for luck,
listened for the voice of the clam,
smelled it for what smell may reveal,
held it to my cheek in summer.
These gray rings and layers of stone,
the shape of a whale's eye,
old as any desert, place me in time.
Measured against it, the morning, the Hudson River
outside my window are modern and brash;
the star of David, the cross, the hand of Fatima,
are man-made weather vanes.

My old clam stands for periodicity,
is my sweet reminder
of heartbeat and poetry, seasons, tides, music,
all phases of all moons, light-years, menses.
Tomorrow I shall wear it for one of my eyes,
a monocle for my talk on the relationship
between paleontology and anthropology.

Bless Celia, the cat of his middle years,
with her ribbons and hats, her wet tongue,
a single note of Scarlatti, barely heard.
Bless the bobcat that was his in boyhood,
that killed a police dog in battle
on Main Street, Worcester, lost a foot for it
and had to be shot. A child with a leaf in his head
he walked through Scabious devil's-bit,
Marshrag wort, Vernal grass
until the meadows wept. Bless his first garden,
his bird feeder still there after 65 years.
How many of his long forgotten kindnesses
altered history a little?

What a *Luftmensch* he might have been,
his feet barely touching Commercial Street,
dancing home at three in the morning
with an ocean of money!
But how could he face the moon, or the land
beside his house without a garden? Unthinkable.
I think what is written in roses, iris
and trumpet vine is read by the Lord God,
such a place of wild and ordered beauty,
is like a heart that takes on the sorrows of the world,
He translates into all tongues.

Dore Ashton

Kunitz and the Painters

"Mark Rothko was such a restless and impatient soul," Kunitz wrote in a brief memoir. "He never could sit through any kind of meeting. The way he squirmed!" Rothko not only squirmed. He paced. In the midst of a dinner he would light a cigarette, thrust back his chair and, on his gumsoles, pad around the kitchen trailing a stream of smoke. Yet, when Kunitz was there, Rothko paused, listened, and often plunged into discussions from which we all profited. There were a half-dozen other painters in those gregarious old days who relished the opportunity to engage Kunitz in talk, talk, talk. He understood them. As he wrote in "A Kind of Order, A Kind of Folly," he preferred their company to that of poets "who tend to be surly and withdrawn."

If Kunitz was something of a connoisseur, it was because he paid attention. I have an ineffable memory of our first encounter. I was living with my husband, a painter, in a small and rather shabby loft up a narrow flight of stairs. It was sometime in the mid-1950s. Kunitz had just settled down in New York and had somehow broken a leg doing so. Up he clumped in his plaster-cast gait. Then, instead of collapsing into the chair I hastened to offer, he clumped around the studio, face thrust close to the canvases, looking hard. We talked that afternoon for hours. I remember being immensely impressed when he proudly told me that he had planted a thousand trees (or was it five thousand?). I have always associated the determined will that great plantation required with Kunitz's poetic presence in my life, and the lives of my friends among the artists.

Within a matter of months Kunitz had become well acquainted with the most gifted artists around, many of whom were destined to fame as innovative artists of The New York School. (Among those whose company Kunitz sought, and who could be found at long evenings at his home, were Franz Kline, James Rosati, Mark Rothko, Giorgio Cavallon,

Adja Yunkers, Philip Guston, Jack Tworkov and Robert Motherwell.) I think what the painters liked—at least those I knew best, Rothko, Kline, Guston and Motherwell—was that Kunitz was a man who spoke unabashedly about a "moral universe." They too were committed to a point of view of existence—an esthetic—that assumed that their place was in a universe created by art and, of necessity, moral.

Their universe was one of constant transformations. Kunitz, who liked to talk about "shapeshifters," was uniquely equipped to understand them. When, shortly after Theodore Roethke's death in 1963, Kunitz wrote about his poetry, he characterized a poetics that could be easily transposed to the works of several of his friends among the painters: "If the transformations of his experience resist division into mineral, vegetable and animal categories, it is because the levels are continually overlapped, intervolved, in the manifold of tissue." During frequent studio visits, at parties, around the dinner table, in his own baroque garden, or strolling through the streets of the Village, Kunitz exchanged views with the painters and sometimes even engaged in Socratic gadflyism. I have known him to provoke for the sake of discussion and I have often noticed his love of paradox when talking with artists. Although I know that the influence of poets is incalculable, I also know that Kunitz's presence among the artists was "intervolved" and in the manifold of their most precious tissue. There were certainly moments in the lives of painters such as Guston, Rothko and Motherwell when Kunitz's prescient remarks sustained their hand.

Some of those remarks during the 1950s I jotted down. In my own case he once startled me, in 1958, by telling me that art critics exaggerated their roles and that they must "give back the man to the work." With a touch of irony that was not lost on me, he reminded me of the value of the quotidian criticism of Sainte-Beuve. During the same year

he and I talked a great deal about Mark Rothko, whom
Kunitz then saw as "a primitive, a shaman who finds the
magic formula and leads people to it." Although Kunitz
was the poet who, as he recently said, understood that "the
way backward and the way forward are the same," and
whose own work so wondrously restores the mythic voice,
he never permitted himself to escape the contingent. In
1960 standing in the corner of my kitchen with Guston and
Rothko he piqued them, saying: "The artist must come back
from his escape into myth and permit himself to be polluted.
He must read newspapers." In those days he pondered the
distinctions between image and icon, and warned against
the production of false icons. He also had a healthy disdain
for the *tummlers* of the art world beating away at their crude
drums. "The artist goes from *his* own center out to a
periphery—as far as he can, but always from his own center,
not the center of some school or pack," he told us in 1959.
Yet, as he said in a public lecture a couple of years ago,
"Every work of art of any interest must be considered as
an event." When he peered close, Kunitz made his friends
among the artists feel as if they had created an event—a
rare and fortifying feeling. I think that the particular artists
with whom he was most in communion were exceptionally
thoughtful, constantly questioning the larger issues implicit
in their own work. When he made grand generalizations
they were stimulated. I remember one in particular that
struck me: Art does not attack its age with its opposite, but
applies homeopathic doses of what the age seems to be
demanding until in the end the age dies of nausea. For
Philip Guston, whose restlessness Kunitz well understood,
such a pronunciamento resounded. Guston was about to
inaugurate a new age after administering his own powerful
homeopathic dose.

Guston's caricatures of Kunitz—he made several—fear-
lessly stress the thrust of his large and curious nose and the
humor of his intense but skeptical gaze. Caricature was

something Kunitz and he understood together. So many others were so bloody earnest that they could never see its virtue. But probably it was Kunitz's willingness to talk about the poets Guston devoured, such as Gerard Manley Hopkins ("the taste of myself in all things") and William Butler Yeats, that attached Guston to Kunitz. During those hard years of the 1960s Guston understood and needed the voice of ancient and tragic wisdom, a voice he found in Kunitz in such lines as:

Within the city of the burning cloud,
Dragging my life behind me in a sack,
Naked I prowl, scourged by the black
Temptation of the blood grown proud...
("Open the Gates")

Kunitz felt artistic affinities with certain painters. A couple of years after Rothko's death he told me that he had been moved by the grandeur of Rothko's work, by its rhetoric of color. "I felt definite affinities between his work and a kind of secrecy that lurks in every poem—an emanation that comes only from language." Kunitz was one of the few men of letters in America who could respect the secret language of the painter; the painter's incarnation of meaning in the language of paint—a language that resists translation but is nonetheless a language.

Probably, though, it is simply Kunitz's capacity for faith that inspires artists. To this day he believes in art. Just a few months ago I had a letter from a young painter telling me that a visit from Kunitz had kept her going for months. If I ask what it was about that visit, and all the other studio visits, I think I can say that it was Kunitz's confirmation of the value of what painters do. His is a mind that, as Coleridge said, "feels the riddle of the world, and may help unravel it." For painters of a contemplative, let's even say romantic, temperament, Kunitz fulfills a great hunger. He proffers a Borges-like view of existence as "a giant web of

21

interconnected filaments that if touched, the whole web trembles"—an ideal vision that many, many painters strive to realize in their works.

Yes, I think, finally, that it is Kunitz's faith that inspirits other artists, and most of all painters. And, perhaps, his wisdom. I was on a plane with him last spring and told him I'd just read an essay by Norbert Weiner in which he predicted that eventually computers could be made so accurate that even a man, rendered into the quantified computer language, could be completely communicated. Kunitz smiled his small smile and answered, "Yes, perhaps, but not a man who could write Dante's *Inferno*."

Cleopatra Mathis

Dancer Among the Constellations

I run for change,
to learn the art of *now* and *wait,* to love
what's not a part of me—
fall's multitude of green, fall's rain,
I give up what the trees release:
sheer will and the time it takes
to understand regret, that whole music
in this haphazard season.

I run to leave the girl
whose need I cannot bear,
for the tension in the body's beat and the dissonant
measure of quiet. For the lilac dome
descending and the rising constellations,
a solitude accepted
in the arc of shooting star. I chase

the brother in the body,
for the sake of wick and burning,
for the burning of the breath.
To stop the automatic counting,
free the song from its intent
and the being that contains the dance,
I free the foot thud
and the longing—freed
lightly for once,
as if it meant some careless rest.

This inconstant globe of light, the moon
blurred half among so many shapes:
unlikely swan, the arrow and the goat.
I exchange these candles
for the other's hesitation. And walk away—
exchange the passionate word

for sweat: this washing out of me,
seed and the salt, anonymous
heat of any flesh,
and nobody's hand for comfort or intent.
I run for the closed
throat insisting, the clenching
in the waist, movement
as if there were no halt.
And for the far-off
figure of the runner,
flexed arm and fist, the rising
under these brief clothes—our bodies
mutual as they empty. Even from this distance
those leaps are my own.

For Once

no accounting, no scheme
to arrange or give up. You, running,
find nothing to run for, and without substitute

turn from sex, from the ceaseless
gathering, from the weed-choked pond.
Heat beats the air like water,

beats its thump in you; the stupid
mouth can't get enough in the almighty
fight for air. This path pulls you

where the stream begins. You pace
to the paddle of the water wheel;
you fix its pump and cease: matching

the tension in the hush, then the water's fall...
As if the body were an animal, and you ride it.
As if that struggle were enough.

To an Unborn Child

Quite simply, I gave you up.
I ran and the miles lengthened
in my security of breath; my fear
less the neighbor's dog
than the buckling in my right knee.
Who knows when you began.
Summer gave itself to the beckoning fall;
apples ripened, though hail left them
ruined for market. Later the trees
shrugged them down. Windfall in the rich grass
they drew a tinge of yellow and such flavor
we learned to prefer the fallen,
barely noticing the tiny slug prints and brown
scabs of weather. Survival, after all,
is not an art, only an indication
of how little there is to trust.
I read this week how one child
spun into the hazardous ball of fire
somewhere over alien territory
and perished, a casual occupant
of the wrong plane. Still another,
just down the road, fell
into one of the orchard hives and
died reacting to the common
defense of bees. In this way we all belong
purely to the world.

Because nothing here means safety—
it's all territory we trespass,
and relentlessly. As that speck of you
lived on greed: the determined cells
multiplying to complete their plan.
It is enough to think of you
as I run in the still dark, your kin
cold above me. In that heaven
the stars move through their soliloquies
and the moon repeats. So much repetition
yet the shrug in any nature—as I your mother
would not give up my body to the long pull
of your survival, its futility and need.

Runner on Ridge Road

No breath for this. I go under
gasping in a sea of trees.
Giving up whatever set me in motion
I let the downhill take me
into the tamaracks
lit with the constellations of
night rain and sun.
They tremble as they break—
nothing real, these prisms and nebula

scattering before me.
Half-lights in the permanent
dusk of the greenish air, the birches
pull me deeper in.
It is the one brown trunk among them

26

that I see last: the deer,
still as earth, though he is
more sea elk than real—waterstalk,
forcing calm in those depths.
Forcing me back to real water,
real marsh: my cedar playhouse, its branch
caught in the cypress, and the dead
who swung there with me.
And I am shaking
more than when I let myself fall
to the pond bottom soaked with leeches.
Enough to provide

the brother who hunted, a clean hunter
who taught me to shoot when the bullet
sees its mark and the deer
is down in one pure shudder.
In some of us, love is not much different
from fear, and fear provides
accuracy, as precision for the deer
means to keep running
or to stand perfectly still.

We stare, held for the instant
by the multitude of surfaces,
underwater drifters
threaded by a little sun.
He's waiting me out, the great body
made of darkness
the light cradles and invades.
Like a stilled dancer
he goes on standing, like a gift
given self to self. I take him in,
leaping and climbing back up to the road.
As though chased by my provider,
my twin among ghosts, and this time
consenting.

Louise Glück

Four Dreams Concerning the Master

1. The Supplicant

S. is standing in a small room, reading to himself.
It is a privilege to see S.
alone, in this serene environment.
Only his hand moves, thoughtfully turning the pages.
Then, from under the closed door, a single hazelnut
rolls into the room, coming to rest, at length,
at S.'s foot. With a sigh, S. closes the heavy volume
and stares down wearily at the round nut. "Well," he says,
"what do you want now, Stevens?"

2. Conversation with M.

"Have you ever noticed," he remarked,
"that when women sleep
they're really looking at you?"

3. Noah's Dream

Where were you in the dream?
    The North Pole.

Were you alone?
    No. My friend was with me.

Which friend was that?
    My old friend. My friend the poet.

What were you doing?
    We were crossing a river. But the clumps of ice
    were far apart, we had to jump.

Were you afraid?
    Just cold. Our eyes filled up with snow.

And did you get across?
    It took a long time. Then we got across.

What did you do then, on the other side?
   We walked a long time.

And was the walk the end?
   No. The end was the morning.

4. Conversation with X.

"You," he said, "you're just like Eliot.
You think you know everything in the world
but you don't believe anything."

Bruce Smith

Silver and Information

An obituary has more news than this day,
brilliant, acid yellow and silver
off the water at land's end. The disparate
prismatic things blind you as they fin
their way across the surface of the water.
This light cannot inform you of your dying.

Fish of lustrous nothing, fish of desire,
fish whose push and syllable
can make things happen,
fish whose ecstatic hunger
is no longer news, and fish whose mouth
zeroes the multitudes, the hosts
who wait for their analogies
and something nice to eat, the billions
the waves commemorate in their breaking
down to their knees on the shore,
their cloacal sound. Now
how can I stay singular?
How can even one part die
when I split and split
like the smallest animal
in the ocean until I'm famous
in my dismemberment, splendid
in my hunger, and anonymous—
so that naming one
is like naming one runnel
the sea, or one drop of blood
the intoxicating passion?

I keep the multitudes in mind
when I hear daily that one
has murdered another. A news
more silver than given,

more light than anything
captured. And I hold them all
in mind—the fulgence, the data,
and the death, or else I lose it,
that package of slippery fish,
that don't die exactly but smell
in a heaven so low we can hear
the moans and feel the circles
and bite in each cell.

One Note Rage Can Understand
—Louise Bogan

To reduce the monster to myself,
in order to scratch where it itches,
I go down to the water and listen
for my name in the waves of the bay.
I go down with the commonest surname
and half my allotted threescore years
and ten to hear what I can
in the concussive thuds off Race Point
at the cusp of America. In the agitation,
in the perjuries, in the gnats and flies,
in the middle of my life
at land's end, I hear
the churned other word.
Whose it sounds like
or *bruise*—a question in the descent,
an erasing statement in the sweep
back to sea that is nothing
but the breath tuned to groans
then cushioned in the utterance

by all we stand on, an anxious
susurrus of history and crushing
rhapsody that is not my name or yours.

Snow on the Ocean

You can prepare for the fall,
its lack of innocence, its bright load,
as if in the scheme of things
you've been given something—
these accomplishments
of air before the cold
paradise of winter
where no fruit falls.
You can prepare all summer for this
and the extravagant chemical changes—
the maple flaming scarlet to rust
to what? It's beneath you
to see its apostasy, its folding.
You can prepare for this
hanging and appleing

but not for this: snow
on the ocean, water in all three forms—
ghost, glass, and what slips
between our fingers, what dissolves
and hugs our forms. Just this much—
a splash in a shot glass,
an inch in a bath, the human
lull and relish of it—
can leave us beautifully used,

almost shoreless, as we pass through
the gills of this planet
with the wrong name,
this earth, whose one season
is the improvident presence of water.

Marie Howe

Menses

This fullness in my breasts and belly
     will ache until it goes away
breaking down like sludge running through
     the rushing gutters, this tenderness
impossible to bear, like a love
     for everything that never was. Outside
my window, even the trees look incredulous,
     as if they had just remembered
their terrible forgetting, and all week,
     apart from you, the snow falls heavily
mixed with inconstant dirty rain.

I wait, and watch a single robin step
     among the paper plates that lie
face down where the fraternity boys
     have left them, smeared with ketchup,
mustard, bits of soggy rolls, and wonder
     how one seed can erupt into
a hungry vine, spitting morning glories.
     This afternoon, I'll cook eggs
for lunch until they are white and solid
     and dead enough to eat.

What is permitted me is only a sure dull sorrow,
     and a sense of skittering on the very
edge of things, about to fall again,
     grateful and sadly deliberate as rain.
You call from the farm to tell me three
     lambs are born, black and bleating
in their stall. The ram that will not breed
     will be sold for meat, only the ewes
will be kept and nurtured and named.
     I cry for no reason and plead with you,
name them Mercy, Patience.

Death, the Last Visit

Hearing a low growl in your throat, you'll know that it's started.
It has nothing to ask you. It has only something to say, and
it will speak in your own tongue.

Locking its arm around you, it will hold you as long as you
    ever wanted.
Only this time it will be long enough. It will not let go.
Burying your face in its dark shoulder, you'll smell mud and hair
    and water.

You'll taste your mother's sour nipple, your favorite salty cock
and swallow a word you thought you'd spit out once and be
    done with.
Through half closed eyes you'll see that its shadow looks
    like yours,

a perfect fit. You could weep with gratefulness. It will take you
as you like it best, hard and fast as a slap across your face,
or so sweet and slow you'll scream give it to me give it to me
    until it does.

Nothing will ever reach this deep. Nothing will ever clench
    this hard.
At last, (the little girls are clapping, shouting) someone has pulled
the drawstring of your gym bag closed enough and tight.   At last

someone has knotted the lace of your shoe so it won't ever
    come undone.
Even as you turn into it, even as you begin to feel yourself stop,
you'll whistle with amazement between your residual teeth
    oh jesus

oh sweetheart, oh holy mother, nothing nothing nothing
    ever felt this good.

Robert Hass

Broken Song

I loved to watch that woman sew
Who let her hair grow long for show.
Riddles are needles
And plainly said is thread.

The world dissolved her body in an instant.
Time soured and the light was scant.
Riddles are needles
And plainly said is thread.

And music was invented. The cracked eye
Watered, the throat gargled *plié, plié.*
Riddles are needles
And plainly said is thread.

Birds savaged one another's nests.
The grass was foul with shadow of her breasts.
Riddles are needles
And plainly said is thread.

Death and art made their compact then.
The sky burned, the air was thin:
The needle furious,
The thread thickened and glistening
As it turned in her keening,
Infant's-breath lightness of body.
Absent now, imagined there wholly.

David Ignatow

The Wedding

You are floating in the warmth
of this personal affection for yourself
you do not often experience
because it is difficult to arrange
a meeting with yourself that will not be
interrupted by events that you yourself
will have interposed, but when you have
accomplished it by dodging every trick
you can devise to avoid this meeting
you are relieved and confidential
with yourself, especially about the fears
that kept you from this meeting. Here
you are then together. How good it feels,
like bride and bridegroom alone
at last after the wedding.

The Value of a Song or a Cry

You're in a swamp up to your thighs.
To get out you have to fling yourself
upon a flat board that will resist suction
if you have a board handy. Upright,
you keep going down. Make a song
of it, make it float out
of the swamp for someone to come
running. Cry aloud, startle
the birds and the leaves
of the overhanging trees
just beyond your reach
for a reason, a good reason

you want to believe,
and let someone come running
even after you sink out of sight
your hand upraised
and let them bury you
decently,
not as an accident in nature.

The Daguerreotype

Your father at twenty, mustachios,
high buttoned shoes, tight suit,
stands one foot forward, cane planted
in front of him, hand gripping it
firmly, "I know my cane and I know
at what I'm looking, being photographed:
my passport to the world I stand in fear of,
except I have my bold style."

You ran errands for him,
delivering meat, chickens, eggs
in the snow before schooltime.
In the dark before going to bed
you make the rounds again, taking orders
for the morning. A bird lying in the gutter
you stuff into your pocket, hoping
to revive it with your warmth,
later to bury it in a hole you dug
for it, brushing dirt back in
to cover the body. You will not defy
the world, nor make a showcase of it
for your pride. Your father works

a butcher shop and your mother too
waits on customers and grows angry
and tired and ill of the damp floor.
Your father, neat and small, staggers out
of the icebox, a whole side of beef
on his shoulder.

Susan Mitchell

The Falls at Otter Creek

As a child I fed it the burned grass growing
by the side of the bridge, I threw stones
instead of myself, bottle caps
dug from wood, strings of tar, and keys
pressed so flat by trucks
no one could walk anymore through the doors they opened.
Day after day I let out my breath, umbilicus torn
from my mouth, and when breath failed,
garlands of smoke and ashes. I dangled
words, reeling them out and in,
saliva and spittle, shards of blood, black
phlegm coughed from bone. And when words failed
I tried snow, I tried light and hush
and what one mouth sucked from the other.
The rain taught me how simple it was,
how the water darkened for a moment, dimpling
like flesh when I touched it
pulled to the side of roads in summer,
the gnats that I sweated out,
the faint murmur of water
that never left me. And before it spilled,
the body thinned, curling to the merest transparency
of flesh, as if to let go
it had to assume the color of air
or wings on fire.
And sometimes what I heard
was darker than any water imagined, a shuddering
older than blood, and deeper,
as if an organist had let out all
the stops, some failed composer playing my song
in a lounge where those who crowded in
came for the twofers, Manhattans stirred like
salad dressings from mixes, not the music.
I think that composer is playing tonight

out of joy, out of the abandoned car wash
where I waited after school,
I think he is playing the stops that can mimic
everything, success and love, as well
as the boy dancing near the bar,
his face pulled down like a cap. Thumbs hung
in his red and black checked suspenders,
he leans out stunned beyond
the last syllables of grass where
the voice coils its smoke in rank wisps.
And doesn't he dream it too—
climbing the falls some night
skimming out over rocks and the slippery squeak
of moss, over the movie house boarded up,
over the shop windows dismembered of
their mannequins and tinsel,
knees wrapped tightly around the spray
as around a lover, the slender shoots of breath
straining to unravel, so that
years later driving home from work
someone might stare at his name
spraypainted red and larger than life,
the initialed heart still
dripping on the graying cement
of the overpass where he once stuttered up
amazed and dizzy and alone.

Dirt

It might be true
the story that Daniel Boone slept in a cave
not far from Rockville, Indiana.

It might even be true that the cave he slept in
was the one I ran into during a downpour.
Striking a match, I saw BOONE
carved into hard rock.
Of course, anyone could have done that.
I could have done it myself.
Once, camping near Rockville, I came on the skeleton
of a dog. It had recovered its cleanliness
from the black soil
the way flowers recover after a rain.
Sometimes I'm afraid of what I'll find, not
animal bones or the arrowheads
that turn up everywhere,
but the skeleton of a man,
someone who listened to the soil
asserting itself day after day until his bones
became tools for digging him deeper.
I've had a stone scraper reach into my hand
like another hand wanting me
to feel my way back to it.
I felt the grass growing westward
starting to pick up speed
like an animal running for the sheer
joy of running,
and I thought of Boone following his traps,
each trap biting deeper
into the green absence of prairie.
I understood
his wanting to keep it for himself,
the space that lay down with him each night,
breathing into his face.
On the prairie night asserts itself like a smell.
One night I heard the prairie talking,
it said *itself, itself* over and over.

I lay there thinking of all the disguises
a body can take: stone, stump, vine, root.
I listened to the wind
turning over in my sleep and I prayed
to be unremembered as the dirt
that cakes the nails of men and women as they work.

Tom Sleigh

Jenny Fish

Junior High Prom
Brigham City, Utah

Slender Jenny Fish, you danced with your Dad,
A man dressed darkly with a black bow-tie.
He danced much closer than the rest of us did,
Each step cutting a sharp geometry,

His boxstep divvying the dance floor into squares,
As he held your hand high, the silver sleeve
Tensing like a slot machine lever;
And in your face was no pleasure, just nerve

To keep your pride up, to hide your outrage.
Your dress brushed the tops of your low-heeled shoes
While you followed your Dad as if the edge
Of an abyss widened from the slow-slow

Quick-quick of your pace. We boys gawked amazed,
Unbelieving of the golden chain that yoked
Your glasses to your neck, the flat bodice
Of your dress, so unlike the tissue-padded

Poke of other girls. But how you could dance
Compared to our shambling, how darkly male
Your father looked, as your passion grew dense
And seemed to light your face against the cool

Hard blackness of his suit. None of us dared
For long to watch the turns he would exact,
And, as I remember, I was scared
Before that bleak paternal fact,

Whose every step was a command
Obeyed with furious precision,
As above you, in a fist, your twining hands
Clenched with draconian affection.

Hilda Morley

The Candles

It is the silence which surrounds them that makes me
peaceful,   a depth
around them:
         when I come upon them,
                      forgetting
they are there,   lit-up & pointing
upwards
        as if they were
praying.
       It is their steadiness—
especially the smaller of them which
burn gravely,
         are more full
              Only
the tall ones seem to
be endangered—having ventured
so far, so high—
         danger
can find them easily.
          They are open
to the winds that buffet them.
             Even
their own breathing can become uncertain,
                  causing them
to waver,
        their own heartbeat
fitful, strenuous,
         a fever
of longing,
        sometimes even
a longing to go backward,
           falter,
to give up whatever they were

made for,
   that persisting.
But how short their moment
of despairing:
    space deepens
around them,
    for the shape of
their continuing is faithful,
      a sweeping,
      a stretching out of
distance in tenderness.
      It is not
a single word that they are saying
over & over,
    not a salutation,
not even a blessing.
     It is that all languages
are fused together here,
     breathed out
in this light & forgotten.
     The body
rising from its sleep, out of
the caves of its own darkness is given
its height in continuance,
     the wick blown upon,
the tip shaken, light uneven.
      Silence dug out
deeper than a tree-root,
     so deep there is
no word yet, only a
fragrance.
   Something is guarded—
neither evening nor morning
      something watched over here,
but not a phrase yet, not a syllable.

Grace Schulman

Carrion

The chipmunk's carcass lay flat on a stone
stair that leads to rooms above the shed.
Hind legs, a tail, a strand of wine-red beads
and innards, showed whose body it had been.

One step above the corpse, a yellow cat
unfurled, his eyes half closed, guarding his kill
Caretakers had fed him well, and still
the animal had craved some swifter prey.

The cat himself, ill-used, had been abandoned.
Boarded at stables here to calm the horses,
he was released after the racing season
passed, and found a temporary home

on this estate. Later he would be free
to forage in the woods. The horse he soothed
"Would make a good breed mare when racing days
were done," the auctioneer said. Rings of grief:

Scissors, paper, rock, I sang as a child.
Scissors cuts paper that covers rock
that pulverizes scissors. Still I'm held
in that small circle, flaying being flayed.

Small fingers whipped my wrist: bland-mannered Catherine
was *paper.* I, being *rock,* would strike
my dearest Anne, with flimsy yellow hair
for being *scissors.* So the wheel turned, and turns.

I touched the chipmunk's glittering cadaver,
then buried it. The cat quivered to rise,
warning my hand that touched the prize he murdered.
Beyond the steps, a spruce raised votive candles.

Walking through double rows of junipers,
that day, I glanced away from cruelty,
or so I tried: a hawk warped on the wind
called back the day I watched a herring gull

circle to land, scoop up a turtle, soar
upward again and drop it to crack its shell.
My neighbor shot the gardener who denied
they ever loved, and who was seen at Bill's

drinking bourbon with another woman.
"She seemed too old to care, too mild to kill.
She won't get off," a villager remarked,
sadly, I thought. I never knew the killer,

had seen her only, taut as a dry leaf
someone had kicked on the ground, chilly, austere,
skin of worn porcelain, her lean body
angular in stride, flexed, as in flight.

That night my feet, my elongated thighs
stiffened and went cold, my body turned
upward, and my carrion entrails
flickered below my eaten chest, my eyes.

Galway Kinnell

Driftwood from a Ship

It is the white of faces from which the sunburn has suddenly been
   scared away.
It has the rounded shoulders of those who fear they will pass the
   rest of their days alone.
The final moments of one it couldn't hold up—possibly the cook,
   who possibly could neither cook nor swim—have been gasped
   into it.
The black residue inside the black holes—three set close together,
   three far apart, three close—remembers the hammer blows'
   downward stages, which shined nine nails permanently into
   their vanishing places.
A planes' long, misericording *shhhhhhhhhs* long ago soothed away
   the halo fragments the sawmill's circular saw had tormented
   across its planes.
The pebbles it rubs itself into fuzz up all over it a first beard, white
   right from the start.
Its grain cherishes the predicament of spruce, which has a trunk
   that rises and boughs that fall.
Its destiny is to disappear.
This could be accomplished when a beachcomber extracts its heat
   and resolves the rest into smoke and ashes; or in the normal
   way, through combined action of irritation and evanescence.

W. S. Merwin

Nine
(for Koun Yamada)

First month of the year
  the eleventh day
  with its anniversaries

as you were flying home
  into your language
  cloud voice clear word

I planted a clump
  of giant golden bamboo
  when I stood up the rain had come

Gregory Orr

The Tree

1

These surgings not merely sheathed in flesh
but in the mind where lust
is a helix of vine twining
death's trunk—twinned upthrusting
whose mingled foliage makes
a tapestry more green than black.

2

The word does not share
the world's flaw ("leaf"
is complete, unscarred
by insect or wind-tossed twig),
yet it is an essence
that implicates the world
as a wound implies a body.

3

Each day the web made new—pattern
of line and space;
                          no matter
how tight the weave, emptiness
at the center; no matter
how vast the space, the furthest filaments,
held fast to leaf and twig, are love.

4

Autumnal language: fullness and falling
away from the tree of self,

death with a future like seeds
in fruit...
                In spring I kneel
to find it: that word in earth
extending downward one root,
upward one leaf...
                Not eyes
discover it, nor even fingers
touching and probing mud, but
mouth and tongue—to taste
this world on lips
where, for that instant, the world lives.

Peter Davison

Crossing the Void
(for Stanley Kunitz)

I pick my crooked way
across a half-built bridge
past left-behind lunchpails,
rusting wrenches, cables
coiled scattershot
half across the span.
Could my scream be heard?
No, nor anyone catch
a glimpse of a body falling
to the rocks, hammered to pieces
by the brawling stream below.

I count my footsteps toward
the emptiness ahead
with no memory pushing me,
not the milk-scented kisses of childhood,
nor the prickle of revenge,
nor the black hounds of grief.
Against my face
droplets of flannel mist
dash tiny explosions.

Misguided by travel,
I know that without ground
I can hear no music, yet
unless I go on I'll be barred
from footing ashore
in rigging, on bridges,
clambering or crossing. As I approach
the vanishing point, I begin to feel
a half-remembered sickness
as when the waterfilled seaboot
pulls down, and then the list,
heave and plunge
of sinking planking.

Rose Slivka

Patches and Portraits

So it finally comes to this: the ordinary life, dailiness, day-by-day. Last summer, for an exhibition I curated called "Ordinary and Extraordinary Uses," Stanley Kunitz sent me a sink strainer he had made by hand for his kitchen on West 12th Street. It was wonderfully made and would last long after the sink around it and the pipes below had disintegrated. It was ordinary, so ordinary, basic and obvious, there was no way for it to become a metaphor for anything but its self. It was one of the two objects the museum declined to show, the other one being a packing crate Connie Fox had used over the years to send her paintings over the world. It was a trifle more sophisticated than the strainer simply because it had been more places and showed it. But Stanley Kunitz's handmade kitchen sink strainer made of steel sheet, each hole punched, drilled, sanded and polished by hand, was so plain, unadorned and unadornable, each hole made by hand one at a time, each a considered thought accompanied by the act, to fit a freak-sized drain for which ready-made strainers were no longer being made, therefore worthy of the Kunitz time and attention, his sense of craft. And ordinary, ordained to receive the full imprint of a meticulous hand.

On New Year's Eve of 1985, Stanley gave each of his guests a copy of his new poem, "Passing Through," written on the occasion of his 79th birthday, a poem so lighthearted, filled with light and air, easygoing and tasty, I wanted to take it into my mouth whole like I do the yolk of my two-minute egg. The poem was on a cheap piece of Xerox paper and after we read it, we could throw it away. The words of the poem are everyday words, and if I tried to say what it is all about, it would be like trying to describe the pattern of a fingerprint listening. It's as delicate and slippery as that bubble of egg yolk in my mouth. It is balanced on a wink.

It has the patience of an herb. It is funny. Hilarious. And it could have been written at no other moment of his life. In these last years he becomes more simple and transparent, more sure, more magnificent, more tender, more kind, more of a grieving spirit, more tragic, more funny.

His wife, Elise Asher, the painter and herself a poet, knows the words to every popular song of the thirties, forties and fifties, every song to which we danced the foxtrot and the jitterbug, every song for which we remembered a boyfriend, good times and bad, an event in the tumult by which we grew up, the songs that go ringing in my head all the time telling me what I am really thinking when I think I'm not thinking. Before Elise, I think Stanley's ears were tuned only to the majestic.

I love to talk with him at martini time around 5:30 P.M., when he stops work to have his ritual two martinis before cooking dinner (he is an excellent cook) and then going back to work at midnight. After midnight, he is connected to that other sphere—that invisible place he is always seeming to see. This afternoon, we speak about the power of the ordinary, about daily life, to believe in it and ordinariness as being expressive. "Now that I have become ordinary at last," he says. Kunitz the gardener says, "I need these day-by-day satisfactions." To passing strangers who admire his garden in Provincetown, he says he is the hired hand. He speaks not easily, each word a caring utterance coming out of endeavoring, aspiring sounds of breath, and body struggle, each word surrounded by voicings, uh's, m-m-m's, the voice music in the river of thought, each word light on the water of the river. I love his note, the feel of it, always feeling the life of perishing things.

Four years ago we talked about that and form for a piece in *Craft International* that I called "On the Labyrinth of Form and the Turning of Worms." He said, "Poetry is rooted in the wisdom of the body." The body, he says, is made of its physical matter, its spirit and its intellect. Growing old means that as the physical wanes, spirit and intellect become stronger in compensation, and actually feed the body. Stanley cheers me on to enjoy and enjoin the gathering of powers and to find it in the language where it already lives inside us. We talk about the strangeness, the miracle of being, of being alive at all.

My son, Marc, came then to take pictures of Stanley talking and thinking, to watch his face. The human face in thought, the thinking face, the talking face is probably the most beautiful thing in the world. Quiet faces engrossed in inner speech are exquisite. Marc tried to capture the special quality of the Kunitz face in contemplation, the deep loneliness in his face. I have yet to see a good photograph of his face as it moves in language from that vast interior place. So, for his 80th birthday, I would try to paint his portrait: Portrait of the Poet Stanley Kunitz, hand-painted in oil by Rose Slivka. I would paint his thinking talking face, the long lids, the sad bulging eyes, the puffy sagging bags under the eyes, the heart-shaped face, the high cheekbones, the receding chin, firm jaw, aquiline nose, flurry of white hair, fine Warner Baxter-Ronald Colman moustache on the long ridge of his upper lip, his ruddy healthy glow.

Actually, the photograph Marc did of him was quite fine, on the dark side but essential Kunitz, a little rumpled sitting in his living room at Butterfield House, surrounded by the paintings and sculpture and photographs of family and friends, and objects of folk art and fantasy, that so inhabit his and Elise's world. He looks away from us into the distance as if in touch with invisible and mysterious forces. It seems to me a place where there are many winds and stones, very unlike, probably the opposite of, the gardens Kunitz grows here in the outside world. We sit there watching him take that faraway gaze, that *knowing*. That night, my son Marc tells me I look like Stanley Kunitz. Aside from the fact that we both have puffy eyes and bags to go with them, Marc means it as a profound compliment and I am truly pleased. Then, three years later when he comes to Pearl London's workshop to speak to us, Eleanor Alper says the same thing to me. Again I am flattered. I like to think he could have been my older brother, the one who would have shared his secrets and his sins with me.

So, first I would paint him as the poet in his saffron-colored shirt, in the plush chair, with skin tones of shining orange and magenta. I would paint Stanley Kunitz in all his eyes, heavy-lidded and filled with distant and intimate knowing, with light, as his language is now filled with light, an actual physical lightness of weight, as if now, he and everything he needs weigh no more than a teaspoon of salt. His language now is like that of the painters who have aspired to paint light, which means that even color finally takes flight in the radiance. I would try to paint Kunitz like Monet—in a flickering river of strokes in flight, in a series of studies that would try, perhaps unsuccessfully, but would try nevertheless, to capture the essential Kunitz light at 80, like those waterlilies of Monet, like Monet himself.

And so as I continue to paint my portrait of Stanley Kunitz, the poet, I picture the other ordinary Kunitzes implicit in the poet and in the series, each a different aspect of the same painting.

Picture Kunitz: the standup comedian

Not a very good one for wisecracks. But with enough startled innocence to be absurd without having to say much. The words are still too hard to come by, there are still too many lumps and stones in his throat. We would work up an act called "Passing Through." Kunitz is in a hobo outfit (he'd look good in rags), a little Buster Keaton-ish, and I would simply be me, a tall midget, a round stump of a woman, watery and slightly askew, standing on a small step-ladder behind my view camera on tripod taking his portrait as he poses in front of Trump Tower on Fifth Avenue with the throbbing gristle of the very culture beating past us. Since I never seem to have the right clothes and the right clothes never look right on me anyhow, I would be dressed in a black velvet maumau, and try to look as much like George Sand as possible. At a certain point we would do a soft-shoe duet and if we couldn't think of anything to say, we might lean on Jimmy Hoffa for a punchline: "We got our faults. But being wrong ain't one of them."

Picture Stanley Kunitz: the short-order cook

At the Champion Coffee Shop on 12th Street and 6th Avenue, spatula in hand, standing at the grill, black and white checkered chef's pants and white apron, flipping the hamburger over with a flick of the wrist, his left hand on his hip, authority in the gesture as he presses down on the hamburger with the spatula, slides it under, flips the burger on the toasted bun and removes the unit to a plate, a series of gestures so enjoined and flowing as to be like a dance. For a moment, he turns around and we see the face shining and ruddy with heat, eyes inspecting us from under long lids, patience studded with stamina, like diamonds. "Burger," he calls out, his voice a drum-roll among the clatterings.

Picture Kunitz: the corner druggist

At 12th Street and 8th Avenue where I go to discuss my aches and pains and my latest fight with my current husbands, boyfriends, children, etc., he is always there to receive me in his little backroom where he mixes powders in his marble mortar and pestle, and on an old manual Underwood, he types with two fingers. I sit back there with him at night a couple of times a week waiting for him as he takes care of each customer and we sit and talk about my life when he gets back, rarely his, since his seems to be serene and ordered. Yes, I like that. Vitamin C for my cold and blackberry tea, aspirins for my arthritis, Roger and Gallet Sandalwood Bubble Bath and gold eyeliner for my depression. Sometimes he even lets me type his labels.

Picture Kunitz: the janitor

Of the apartment house opposite my house. On warm summer evenings he sits in jeans and T-shirt in front of the seven-story red brick building, keeping his eye on the street. I cross over. I say, "It is June." I say, "Looks like it's going to be a hot day tomorrow." "Yeah," he says. "There's no letup. Looks like it's going to be a hot summer." We are not telling each other anything we don't already know we know. We are not informing each other, elevating each other, reassuring each other. The words don't need to mean what they say. We are voicing and hearing, sounding for each other in the same way as fish go gulp and dogs bark at each other. He sits, his head turned to the west where the sun is setting in the river. I too. I stand there quietly watching the sun set.

It takes one to know one: we lonely and resisting ones, arranging and rearranging thoughts, words, selves, having been born with the affliction of knowing loss, having received at birth the gift for grief. We walk between paper and stone, the sounds of a woman writing the names of our dead over and over, ink on paper, stone on stone.

Tess Gallagher

To Work and Keep Kind

Of the multitude of spoken and unspoken injunctions handed on from parents, teachers, and friends, there are a simple few the heart selects and pursues with an instinctive recognition. My title comes from Stanley Kunitz's plea to the ghost of his father at the end of the poem "Father and Son":

"O teach me how to work and keep me kind."

It is just these necessities that Stanley Kunitz has held out to me over the past twelve years of our friendship.

The character of Kunitz's own work and his dedication to the work of young writers over the years continue to inspire and amaze me. The impression is of an energy not unlike that of the salmon he writes so movingly about in "King of the River":

You would dare to be changed,
as you are changing now,
into the shape you dread
beyond the merely human.

His energy is indeed full of changes, of transformations informed by that final knowledge of our human fatedness, which commands us, as he says in the poem, to "increase and die." His faith in my own endeavors to write poetry and to teach has been a guiding force at the very heart of my writing and living. The luck of this association calls to mind his translation of Anna Akhmatova's lines: "But if I could step outside myself/and contemplate the person that I am/I should know at last what envy is."

The first time I heard Kunitz's name was when Theodore Roethke read aloud to us a Kunitz poem entitled "The Science of the Night" in the spring of 1963. After Roethke's sudden death that summer Stanley Kunitz made his first appearance in my life. He came to the University of

Washington to read his poems in a special program to commemorate Theodore Roethke. It was the fall of 1963. I had just been swept away as only the young can be by the vision of a life dedicated to the writing of poetry. All summer I'd been washing dishes at night in a restaurant. Days I worked in the newsroom of my hometown paper as a reporter and girl Friday, hoping to be able to afford to return to college. On the occasion of Mr. Kunitz's reading, I was dispirited. Sick at heart. Roethke was gone.

When Kunitz was ushered into the packed lecture hall and seated in the chair directly in front of mine, it was as if an emissary from Roethke had suddenly arrived. I was so shaken by the sense of this that I remember thinking I should ask Mr. Kunitz to sign his book of poems for me—a daring act indeed, since I had denied myself such a request of Roethke out of an assumption that this was probably beneath his dignity. But I was too far gone in need to honor such a scruple now. Nonetheless, my hand refused to make the short reach over the back of the chair to proffer the book. I'm laughable to myself in that moment, but caught too by the earnestness of such attachments to those who shepherd anyone's first tottering gestures in the attempt to write. Not until thirteen years had passed would hands extend the same book of poems into those of Mr. Kunitz.

But the voice that gave his poems that day, full of unsentimental consequence and self-mended yearning, seems to have imprinted itself onto my psyche. I know now, as I didn't then, that the deep recognitions I felt had to do most probably with our common search for our fathers. Kunitz's own father had died as a suicide in a public park the spring before he was born. My father was alive, but distanced from me by drinking and spiritual torments that divided him from everyone. While Kunitz attempted to resurrect his father in order to gain the time they'd never had, I seemed pitted against the clock of my father's life in an effort to construct a language of the heart that would, I hoped, reach him and consequently my own life, before it was too late.

By comparison, I had a bounty of time with my father; and because I seized my task so early, I think my poems had time to grow in clarity and finally did give solace to my father. Yet since his death, I've felt closer to the mysterious ramifications of the loss Kunitz must have lived from the start. There is the cold withdrawal at the end of "Father and Son" as the father's ghost turns toward his son "the white ignorant hollow of his face." And, in a similarly eerie moment, the ghost of Abraham Lincoln coexists with a contemporary likeness that bears his "rawboned, warty look,/a gangling fellow in jeans" and then gives way to "that other one/who's tall and lonely." Kunitz has been haunted a lifetime by the sense of one who has been banished forever from the kingdom of the living. Perhaps this is what gives his poems such a strong reserve of mystery—this feeling of presences which have the power to outlast their corporeal forms.

Recently I used the word "mystery" in speaking to a group of writing students in Urbana, Illinois, and they looked at me incredulously, as if I'd just suggested they all dig wells and drink only well water from that day forward. Mystery in poems seemed an anachronism. "I need my grottos," I said. There was a blank look on their faces. At this point I reached for Kunitz's book of essays, *A Kind of Order, A Kind of Folly,* turned to the chapter entitled "Seedcorn and Windfall," and read to them:

> Poets today tend to be clearer—sometimes all too clear. A poem is charged with a secret life. Some of its information ought to circulate continuously within its perimeter as verbal energy. That, indeed, is the function of form: to contain the energy of a poem, to prevent it from leaking out.

It is this sense of a secret inner life which nourishes the poems, signals its taboos and rituals as they limit or instruct access, that I value in Kunitz's poetry and person. Yet this containment never intends to obfuscate meaning arbitrarily. His mysteries arrive without exertion as a natural extension of his spirit finding voice.

In 1973 I was attending classes at the Iowa Writers' Workshop when I purchased Kunitz's translations of Anna Akhmatova. I had so far not found a female poet in English who wholly captured my imagination. Akhmatova, through Kunitz, came powerfully alive for me. I sat at the kitchen table in the small upstairs apartment and began writing the poem "Stepping Outside." It was directed to Akhmatova, telling her how she had allowed me to face some of the hardships of my life through her own example of strength. In a rush of gratitude I typed the poem and sent it off to Stanley Kunitz, whom I had never met.

Having since received many such gifts myself from those who've read my poems or essays, I now understand what a rare thing it was when I took from my mailbox a reply from Kunitz. So often the best intentions to thank or to inquire further toward such volunteer correspondents have been delayed or have escaped me altogether in the rush of travel or teaching. All the more to wonder at the magnanimous reply he made. "Are all your poems this good?" he questioned. "Send me a group. I'm introducing several poets in the *American Poetry Review*." It was to be my poetic debut, the first time a group of my poems would appear in a poetry magazine with a large national circulation. I felt "discovered" and the loneliness of my strivings seemed, at last, to have won an advocate.

Three years later I was able to arrange a meeting when Kunitz accepted an invitation to read his poems at Kirkland College in Upstate New York. I had just joined the teaching staff there. My personal life was a shambles. I was recently divorced from my poet husband and was unsure of what to do next. Kunitz arrived *sans* luggage, *sans* poems. I remember our first task together was to search in the library for periodicals that carried his most recent poems. We talked all the while of Roethke, and I remember a feeling of child-like jubilation on my part—not that of meeting, but of reunion. This visit, crucial as it was, renewed my resolve toward my own writing and confirmed me in the steps I had just taken to leave my unhappy marriage. I cannot do other than think that the fresh reserve of energy that allowed me to leave America for Ireland shortly afterwards had something to do with the encouragement Kunitz had given me. There I was to write most of the poems that formed the heart of my second book, *Under Stars*.

Since then an intimacy so akin to that of father and daughter has developed that I fear mentioning it as such. Maybe I'm afraid it is spell that allows such an inheritance. Also, I know I'm not the only beneficiary. I have good sisters in his affection—Louise Glück, Carolyn Forché, Cleopatra Mathis, Mary Oliver, Olga Broumas—my friends and some of the leading poets of my generation. And there are others—Michael Ryan, Daniel Halpern, Robert Hass, Gregory Orr—writers who have likewise benefited from his wisdom and support.

I remember his journey to the Northwest in 1978 for a writers' conference in Port Townsend, Washington, and how he drove with me to my birthplace an hour away to go fishing with my father and me for salmon. He caught a beautiful fifteen-pound salmon that day, and we photographed it near my mother's rhododendrons before taking it back to Port Townsend for our supper. My mother led Stanley around her flower garden and they developed an instant rapport—she reciting the names of plants and he often recognizing something aloud before she could tell him, thereby presenting, as unobtrusively as possible, his own credentials as an accomplished gardener.

At some point they got into a lively, but friendly, argument about which was the oldest known tree in the world. My mother insisted it was the Bristlecone Pine. Stanley argued that it was the *Metasequoia glyptostroboides,* commonly known as the Dawn Redwood. *"Pinus aristata,"* my mother declared, and stood firm. Over the next several years I passed clippings from various newspapers and gardening journals back and forth between them proving one or the other case. Clearly neither was going to lose this debate. My mother had proudly displayed her own Bristlecone Pine to Stanley before he left, and this caused Stanley to say to me at the end of one of our visits in the East, "I'd like to give your mother a Dawn Redwood. Sometime I will."

After my father's death in 1982, the time seemed appropriate. The idea of the tree had accumulated sufficient significance. I followed instructions and went to the nursery to make the purchase for Stanley. The next day, to my mother's delight and surprise, a truck arrived with the Dawn Redwood. It was planted a little distance from its adversary, the Bristlecone Pine. This seems to have settled the contest between them, and in its place are my mother's ministrations toward the tree itself, referred to now simply as "Stanley's tree."

I tell this story to commemorate the longevity of the man himself as we celebrate his poetry, criticism, and many personal gifts to the entire literary community in his eightieth year, and to bring us back to kindness, without which the work we do would be bereft of its deepest rewards. Stanley Kunitz's gifts to me as I've sketched them briefly here amount to a debt that can only be answered with love, and that isn't an answer—it is more like two trees, each reputed to be the oldest living tree in the world, growing silently upward, side by side.

Elise Asher

Downward Resurrection

Still pinioned under rock I felt my will hoisted,
Long loamy roots dredged up through punctured bone,
The entire wreck of me dragged into the gleaming air
  and hurled.
On my own then soared over plateglass, city clock,
  past seasons;
And craning my tour above all worldly sound, there
In the high hung haze were you, twin struggling bird,
All brine and bleeding gaze and gifted—
All shy, sly, and deliberately loving—
Knowing well we'd join though both still smarting;
Till down the slippery light we sped together,
A pair of kites until we hit the earth
Where once again our ways would walk the weathers,
Your salty self recovered, your old powers:
Those fertile windstrewn words, those raging flowers.

Joyce Carol Oates

Hermit Crab

Legend,
or mere gossip?—
the crab
that, homeless,
appropriates
the shells of creatures
who have died
and rotted away.
"Isn't it ignoble,"
the crab is asked,
"to have no shell,
no defining structure,
of your own?"

"All shells,
all structures,
define"—
the crab's
dignified reply.

And this too
in an appropriated
cadence.

Tomas Tranströmer

Six Winters

1.

In the black hotel a child's asleep.
And out there: the winter night
where the wide-eyed dice roll.

2.

An elite of dead turned into stone
in Katarina churchyard
where the wind shakes in its armour from Svalbard.

3.

One winter during the war when I was ill
an enormous icicle grew by the window.
Neighbor and harpoon, a memory without clue.

4.

Ice hangs from the edge of the roof.
Icicles: the Gothic upside down.
Abstract cattle, udders of glass.

5.

On a siding an empty railway carriage.
Still. Heraldic.
With journeys in its claws.

6.

Tonight a snowy mist, moonlight. The jelly-fish moon itself
floats before us. Our smiles
are homeward-bound. Enchanted alley.

Translation by Göran Malmqvist

Yehuda Amichai

Instructions for a Waitress

Don't remove the glasses and plates
from the table. Don't rub
the stain from the cloth. It's good to know:
people were here before me.

I buy shoes which were on another man's feet.
(My friend has thoughts of his own.)
My love is another man's wife.
My night is "used" with dreams.
On my window raindrops are painted,
in the margins of my books are notes by others.
On the plan of the house in which I want to live
the architect has drawn strangers near the entrance.
On my bed is a pillow, with
a hollow of a head now gone.

Therefore don't clear the table:
It's good to know
people were here before me.

Translation by Harold Schimmel

Bohdan Boychuk

Late Spring

In 1980
spring was late
in Georgia.

Only one bare tree
that I passed
had some buds
pushing through the bark,
like white blisters
bursting on the wind.

On my way back,
I failed to notice
that tree.

And I realized
that I was late into my life,
walking out of the landscape
and entering into myself.

Translation by David Ignatow and Bohdan Boychuk

A Noon

Under the hot sun
the fields swell;
women
sticky with sweat
bend over their sickles
and tilt the sunburnt jugs

of their breasts
sinking into stubble.

Translation by David Ignatow and Bohdan Boychuk

You Came

without knowing why you'll leave

lost your feelings
without knowing why you loved

lost your body
without knowing why you lived

you leave
without knowing why you came

Translation by Mark Rudman and Bohdan Boychuk

Peter Balakian

Clamming at Monomoy

All day on palms and knees
the stink and slime
as if the world's hole
were open for the first time—
the black sand smelling
like the cod's drying belly.

I dug with each finger
like a blood-red headless worm
runneling for some foot
breathing so slow
it's hardly more than stone.

All day my light-tipped hands
crawled for each sharp edge,
each pissing membrane.

And when the sky grew dark
and lowered over my back,
and everything between my
head and knees
was warm and salty,
and my slimy thighs
were dark and full of shells,
I let everything out

and felt the world
dumb and gray
ooze upon the sludge
like an innocent belly—
the hymning ocean
of my one breath.

In the Wide Bay

In the wide bay there is a fish
swimming in circles
all morning in the dark—
a dim ordinary bass which has been swimming
since my Father cast the fissure in the sky—
a fish turning its tail in currents
that alter the wind around my head.

I come to this bay
without rod, net, or blood worms,
a foolish man with a week's hair on my face,
my pockets full of money and gold sinkers—
my nose a sniffing perch
in damp light.

My father came here too
on a day like this in calm November
and watched the poplars on the shore
turn into the bay.

He came alone after dawn
and listened for the herons,
watched the scavenging gulls
in confused circles above his head
and knew the simple fish-eating birds
were smelling him as well.

My fishy breath is like his—
I taste the brine he swallowed as a boy.

Father, father, are you behind me
in the wind that forces me to these rocks;
or are you somewhere in the span
of water between these easy waves
and what I cannot see
beyond the middle of the bay?

Maxine Kumin

Two Photographs

Maryland Agricultural College Livestock Show
Memorial Day, 1924

Blond, wholesome, serene,
their white shirtsleeves rolled,
these boys in white ducks
keep sleek black hogs at their feet,
hogs cleaner than licorice sticks in the sun.
Five haltered calves are also held
in tandem while their names
and pedigrees are said aloud.

Mostly I think about
the unseen mud and manure, flies
and screwworms that connect these boys
and their wildest hopes
poised radiant between two wars
while just out of reach of the lens
in their stained bib overalls
stand the farm laborers

greasy with sweat
and undoubtedly black.

U.S. Army Flying School, College Park, Maryland, 1909

Wilbur Wright is racing the locomotive
on the Baltimore and Ohio commuter line.
The great iron horse hisses and hums on its rails
but the frail dragonfly overhead appears to be winning.
Soon we will have dog fights and the Red Baron.
The firebombing of Dresden is still to come.
And the first two A-bombs, all that there are.

The afterburners of jets lie far in the future
and the seeds of our last descendants, who knows,
are they not yet stored in their pouches?

Arthur Gregor

from *The Poem of Heaven Within*

11.

They come, also in dreams, the mistakes
of every age, wander about in the vast
mist-held fields of their regret, figures
whose minds are gone, who cannot weep,
who come to us that we may weep for them,
so they may fade, by retracing as far as
we can, by digging out from our memory
the cause that caused the error to begin—
o error, error that must plague us
the more that heaven's shine, some com-
prehension of the origin brings into view
the mists wherein they must remain encased,
the torments that may fade but never quite
dissolve, o disconsolate figures
that are to us what misshapen forms
must be to those who brought them forth,
whom they must pity if not love,
or love the more for their complicity
in the emergence of distorted lives.
Nor is it just in dreams where this
disturbance lies. The causes of
disharmony being so many and so old,
to be rid of the great roar of their
demand, the power in the blood, have we
not done, have I not done, as they
would have us do? But the great, the patient source
in us is merciful. It is not asked
that we do any more than we can do.
It is not asked that we be killed by their
attack. Only that we do not favor them.
That we battle, but not be on their side.

14.

A drive to Pontlevoy, past fields
of heather, of corn, past sunflowers tall
as high wheat, each in the vast field turned
as in one huge obedience, toward the sun.
How many drives have there not been,
at midday, or sunset when
the flowers have turned the other way,
to visit friends, meet trains, or just see
the countryside, walk through towns.
How many places have we not seen
that are nowhere now but in reflections,
like the entire ascending side of a town on a hill
in the wide river we drove along
on our way back in the evening, all that had seemed
solid, the trees, lampposts, old walls,
nothing but the watery flow
we possess in the end. The sixteenth-century
abbey, the Sun-king's symbol in stone
above the door where the Dauphin had slept
—added impressions in a stream of
impressions, of pomp
once real, of façades once decorated
for arrival or a death. Only
the look, and no matter how many, there is
only one, only the look that receives,
has received that which is actual,
only the look remains at the end of day.
Appearances, not as fixed and solid
but as flowing, as reflected in
the wateriness of time, as contained
forever in the river that flows
nowhere, that is the view of heaven.

Martha Friedberg

Finally

Finally you are able to love this life.
You distinguish yourself.
You have altered a pattern.

Does it matter you're sixty?
That the winter sun blinds you completely?
Shed the seconal years: sour slippers, the groping
    and over-explaining.

You glisten now in your single achievement.
You kiss yourself wherever your lips will reach.
And you walk with love in a winter rain,

in its warm loosening light;
light dripping in pearls
or like glass fruit from the trees.

Hours and hours you stroll
swinging a shut umbrella,
the blackest bird in the closet.

Does it matter it once was your father's?
The bones of a terrible sadness
are stitched to its wing.

Father

When dreams of a live wife
swam in your arms
you would reach for us

and touch our cheeks to test the flesh.
Yes, we survive.

Children, you'd bellow:
Keep your bowels open. Don't eat trash.
We nibbled in secret.
And grew in the dark
like bulbs in the basement
till you spun us around in the light.
Nobody failed. And nobody passed.

Years you are gone.
We still tremble.
O father, what do I care?
You were a beauty.
Four times you voted for FDR.

Mark Rudman

The Mystery in the Garden
(after a visit to Marion Lerner Levine's studio and her painting in progress, The Mystery in the Greenhouse*)*

The letter pinned to the wall,
unfolding, telling
of forgotten disasters,
sunken ships, desperate messages.
The drawers, yanked out of the chest:
a fragile tilt, an incline,
and everything is askew—
upturned in rows like gravestones.
The bold handwriting,
"I did not expect
this tragedy to occur
while I was here...."
The story hidden inside
the arbitrary forms and shapes
and colors of the past.
The quiet and longing
for a time in the garden:
three women in the garden,
as battleships gather
in the harbor just before
the First World War.
The terrible stillness
that precedes mystery.

It looked so peaceful in the garden
if there had been a door
I would have walked in, a gate
and I would have opened it.

She is standing in a red dress
at the entrance to the Botanical Gardens
in early spring.
Smell of magnolias in blossom,

sticky, hot, white.
Gestures, the sound
of another's voice
in a time when sound mattered.

Railroads, semaphores
in the smoky night,
clang of the garden gate,
and the torn letter, unforgotten.

Arrivals, departures.
Gardens and mazes.

I enter without fear of getting lost,
keen on finding a way.

A way...

It is not a place
from where I would need
to be released to live!
Further and father!

Enter here under the garden's gaze.
Amazed, enter the maze.

To be, finally,
where you have always been.
Enter with delight.

The real past, waiting, this cold spring,
for irises and violets and magnolias.
The mystery unfolding
in the longing of J for J,
anxiety, ancient suspicions:

"don't let him do to you
what he did to me,"
were her words in September, 1934...

Indecipherable signatures.
Cryptic, meticulous vision.

To preserve the actual,
but first to enter
the garden, abandoned,
abandoning all habits
and the sundered doubles
of other habits,
gnawing under the skin
like marbleized light—
to enter, then, without fear
of where you will end.

The real, the actual,
flickering, pulsing,
oblivious to the dampness,
raw and awful,
like the skeleton inside the flesh
wearing away desire,
whirling turmoil out of nothing
and no-things,
not what the eye gathers without the ear,
seared, scarred like the fields,
scored like the sky by fire.

The garden, the rows
of gravestones under the arch
where the ducks hide,
lace, latticework,
flowing
like the spirit reclaimed.

I want the murmuring I hear to become flesh,
to lacerate the air.
Sometimes I imagine the earth is still.
And it takes a cracked cup
with a landscape like this one
running through it
to help the light settle down
where it can see,
through these still lives,
eternity,
glimpsed like lightning
disappearing
over the next mountain,

to wander the forbidden ground.

Sound of all that falling.
Father gone, home alone, flees to the sun.
So long since I have seen the sun.
Can I vouch for what it was?
Would my testimony hold?
Would anyone listen, much less believe?
The sun I love, warming my heart,
warming my hands.
Can't hoard the fire.

Father gone, nobody home,
everything far away
and terrifying, like forked light,
far away, scorching
the rooftiles of the chosen,
and the amber turquoise
stained glass windows
of St. Clement's Church
where I wandered
in a haze of transcendence

that Easter Sunday,
and the women were murmuring,
bright eyes flashing,
laughter flowing,
entering a garden's maze,
aroused, and beckoning:
enter here under the garden's gaze.

Stanley Kunitz, age three

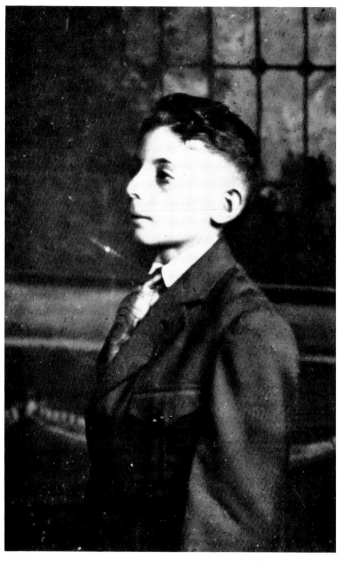

Stanley Kunitz, age thirteen

The Wellfleet Whale, by Paul Resika
Gouache on paper, 1985

The Long Boat, by Elise Asher
Oil on canvas, 1985

Poet and Blank Page, by Robert Motherwell
Collage and acrylic on canvasboard, 1985

Portrait of Stanley Kunitz, by Sidney Simon
Mixed media, 1985

Stanley Kunitz, at Walt Whitman's grave

Ellen Bryant Voigt

The Last Class

Put this in your notebooks:
All verse is occasional verse.
In March, trying to get home, distracted
and impatient at Gate 5 in the Greyhound station,
I saw a drunk man bothering a woman.
A poem depends on its detail
but the woman had her back to me,
and the man was just another drunk,
black in this case, familiar, dirty.
I moved past them both, got on the bus.

There is no further action to report.
The man is not a symbol. If what he said to her
touches us, we are touched by a narrative
we supply. What he said was, "I'm sorry,
I'm sorry," over and over, "I'm sorry,"
but you must understand he frightened the woman,
he meant to rob her of those few quiet
solitary moments sitting down,
waiting for the bus, before she headed home
and probably got supper for her family,
perhaps in a room in Framingham,
perhaps her child was sick.

My bus pulled out, made its usual turns
and parted the formal gardens from the Common,
both of them camouflaged by snow.
And as it threaded its way to open road,
leaving the city, leaving our sullen classroom,
I postponed my satchel of your poems
and wondered who I am to teach the young,
having come so far from honest love of the world;
I tried to recall how it felt
to live without grief; and then I wrote down

a few tentative lines about the drunk
because of an old compulsion to record,
or sudden resolve not to be self-absorbed
and full of dread—
                    I wanted to salvage
something from my life, to fix
some truth beyond all change, the way
photographers of war, miles from the front,
lift print after print into the light,
each one further cropped and amplified,
pruning whatever baffles or obscures,
until the small figures are restored
as young men sleeping.

Cynthia Huntington

These Grapes Are One Hundred Years Old

They do in the air what roots do
in the ground, twisting, grappling,
and clinging
to hold what holds them.

Grass has molded
the yard's hillocks, and padded
the hidden stones under
the ground, surrounded
each with roots and netted dirt.
Stones turn over,
and earth shakes, but roots,
the living, enfold
and try to possess all chaos.
In the air, old vines
grip the sky, lifting

past thè arbor frame,
and it is no longer clear
if it holds them, or if they
have raised the crossed slats
from the ground, and pressed
the squares to the light
where they stand, reaching
up in the quick air.

These grapes are old; my father
tended them thirty years
when he found them gone wild
close to the house he came to late,
already middle-aged, many times a father.

He wanted to live forever; he kept
his house and yard the same

as if another hundred years were certain,
believing the earth could keep on
putting out vines in one place,
that they would raise themselves up
and cling to the sky and still keep
lifting dirt through their branches,
making branches to catch birds
by the moment, that nothing
could stop this from happening
over and over. I think

these are the last. The grapes are small,
nearly black, strong tasting,
with an undertaste of earth.
Their seeds grow large
inside them, the stone that falls
back, weight by which things fall
back. Birds take them up
and let them drop; seeds
fall out of the sky, ticking,
and the wings dip, and rise out of sight.

Hugh Seidman

The Great Ego of the Words

I don't know why the more I gave
the more you feared you would lose.
My greed for you was so simple.
You made me love the world with its greeds.

I don't know why the sun rises or falls
or if the world is too big or too small.

I don't know why we dream till we wake.
When you left I had such greed for the dark.
Was it that your face kept such light?

I don't know why we believe.
I don't know why one word means two things,
or why yes meant no.

I don't know why we need the words.
Today I barely wrote one,
though you had been the dream of each.
Any were enough, if I could come home to you.

But I don't know why for so many
nothing can be said but the words.

And I don't know why so many suffer
in this world, though I know that this poem
has no right to name them.

Yet again, today, as on many days,
when it should have made me dumb
that I did so little for anyone—
still I said your name with such greed.

And how should it be explained
by even the great ego of the words?

Charles Wright

Night Journal II

The breath of What's-Out-There sags
Like bad weather below the branches,
                            fog-sided, Venetian,
Trailing its phonemes along the ground.
                            It says what it has to say
Carefully, without sound, word
After word imploding into articulation
And wherewithal for the unbecome.
                            I catch its drift.

And if I could answer back,
If once I had a cloudier tongue,
                            what would I say?
I'd say what it says: nothing, with all its verities
Gone to the ground and hiding:
                            I'd say what it says now,
Dangling its language like laundry between the dark limbs,
Just hushed in its cleanliness.

The absolute night backs off.
                            Hard breezes freeze in my eyelids.
The moon, stamped horn of fool's gold,
Answers for me in the arteries of the oak trees.
I long for clear water, the silence
Of risk and deep splendor,
                            the quietness inside the solitude.
I want its drop on my lip, its cold undertaking.

C. K. Williams

Dawn

The first morning of mist after days of tiring, unwavering
  heat along the shore: a *breath:*
a plume of sea-fog actually visible, coherent, intact, with
  all of the quieter mysteries
of the sea implicit in its inconspicuous, unremarkable
  gathering in the weary branches
of the drought-battered spruce on its lonely knoll; it thins now,
  sidles through the browning needles,
is penetrated sharply by a sparrow swaying precipitously
  on a drop-glittering twiglet,
then another bird, unseen, is there, a singer, chattering,
  and another, long purls of warble
which also from out of sight insinuate themselves into
  that fragile, fading miniature cloud,
already now, almost with reluctance, beginning its
  dissipation in the overpowering sunlight.

The Park

In that oblivious, concentrated, fiercely fetal decontraction
  peculiar to the lost,
a grimy derelict is flat out on a green bench by the sandbox,
  gazing blankly at the children.
"Do you want to play with me?" a small boy asks another,
  his fine head tilted deferentially,
but the other has a lovely firetruck so he doesn't have to
  answer and emphatically he doesn't,
he just grinds his toy, its wheels immobilized with grit,
  along the low stone wall.

The first child sinks forlornly down and lays his palms
   against the earth like Buddha.
The ankles of the derelict are scabbed and swollen, torn
   with aching varicose and cankers.
Who will come to us now? Who will solace us? Who will take
   us in their healing hands?

William Stafford

Trying to Explain

Manacled on in the cold morning, my watch
tattoos my wrist like those that survived
extermination camps in The War, and
my arm remembers my four years
held inside and even now still imprinted
but never explained enough. You our guards—
often more generous than the prisoners—
what indelible numbers clutch at
your skin this cold morning? Mine
pulses again in a world too various
for indictment but implicated outside
and in. Here is my wrist: mark it
again, you officers who plan to keep on
exterminating whatever enemies
the state can identify. I'll masquerade as human.

May Swenson

Morning at Point Dume

Blond stones all round-sided,
that the tide has tumbled on sand's table,
like large warm loaves strewn in the sun.

Wet pathways drain among them, sandgrains
diamond in morning light.
A high-hipped dog trots toward the sea,

followed by a girl, naked, young,
breasts jouncing, and long fair hair.
Girl and dog in the hissing surf

roister, dive and swim together,
bodies flashing dolphin-smooth,
the hair in her delta crisp dark gold.

The Pacific is cold. Rushed ashore on a wave,
her body blushing with stings of spume
running upslope, the circling dog

leaping to her hand, scatters spray
from his thick blond malamute fur.
Together they twine the stone loaves' maze.

Girl lets her glistening belly down
on a yellow towel on hard hot sand,
dog panting, *couchant* by her side.

Five surfers in skintight black
rubber suits, their plexiglass
boards on shoulders, stride the shore,

their eyes searching the lustrous water
for the hills of combers that build far out,
to mount and ride the curling snowtops.

The sunburned boys in phalanx pass,
squinting ahead, scuffing sand.
Without a glance at the yellow towel

they advance to the sea.
Enormous breakers thunder in.
Falling, they shake the ground.

Robert Pinsky

The Superb Lily

"He burned a great Worlde of Papers before he died,
And sayde, the Worlde was unworthy of them;
He was so superb"—the word

Meant *arrogant* once, the absolute of pride.
    Presidents summered in my home town, once,
        And famous gamblers endowed

Fire houses: the Phil Daly Ladder and Hose
    Survives Lincoln, Grant, Garfield and white,
        Sweet, Lillian Russell.

It's a dump now. But then, Winslow Homer chose
    In his "Long Branch, New Jersey" to paint belles
        On the ocean bluffs, parasols

And bustles in the sun. All dead. "Superb Lily"—
    A name W.C. Fields might call a lady.
        We called it *Swamp Lily* there:

Swollen perennial, that sucked bogs thirstily
    In August, and in the droning air pulled
        Fiery petals back behind

Like arms with linked thumbs to show the throbbing-
    Orange, purple-dotted tissue, moist
        Flamboyant endowment spread

To shoot out glandular dark purses bobbing
    Almost vertical on the springy stamens,
        Phoenix of stagnant water.

Linda Pastan

Ethics

In ethics class so many years ago
our teacher asked this question every fall:
if there were a fire in a museum
which would you save, a Rembrandt painting
or an old woman who hadn't many
years left anyhow? Restless on hard chairs
caring little for pictures or old age
we'd opt one year for life, the next for art
and always half-heartedly. Sometimes
the woman borrowed my grandmother's face
leaving her usual kitchen to wander
some drafty, half-imagined museum.
One year, feeling clever, I replied
why not let the woman decide herself?
Linda, the teacher would report, eschews
the burdens of responsibility.
This fall in a real museum I stand
before a real Rembrandt, old woman,
or nearly so, myself. The colors
within this frame are darker than autumn,
darker even than winter—the browns of earth,
though earth's most radiant elements burn
through the canvas. I know now that woman
and painting and season are almost one
and all beyond saving by children.

Michael Ryan

My Dream by Henry James

In my dream by Henry James there is a sentence:
"Stay and comfort your sea companion
for a while," spoken by an aging man
to a young one as they dawdle on the terrace
of a beachfront hotel. The young man doesn't know
how to feel—which is often the problem
in James, which may have been the problem
with James, living, as he said, *in* the work
("—this is the only thing..."), shaping his late
concerti of almost inaudible ephemerae
on the emotional scale. By 1980,
when this dream came to me, the line spoken
takes on sexual overtones, especially since
as the aging man says it he earnestly presses
the young man's forearm, and in James
no exchange between people is simple,
but the young man turns without answering
to gaze over the balustrade at the ocean,
over the pastel textures of beach umbrellas
and scalloped dresses whose hems brush the sand,
without guessing the aging man's loneliness
and desire for him. He sees only monotony
as he watches waves coming in, and this odd
old man who shared his parents' table on the ship
seems the merest disturbance of the air,
a mayfly at such distance he does not quite hear.
Why should I talk to anyone? glides over his mind
like a cloud above a pond
that mirrors what passes over and does not remember.
But I remember this cloud and this pond
from a midweek picnic with my mother
when I was still too little for school
and we were alone together

darkened by shadows of pines
when with both hands she turned my face
toward the cloud captured in the water
and everything I felt in the world was love for her.

Shirley Kaufman

Happy Endings

I want to write stories with happy endings.
I want to write about the good life.
Even if it's somebody else's. Pliny
had a good life here in his villa.
Better than any life in Rome.
Terraces and porticos, a small hippodrome
for riding, hot and cold baths, gravel paths
between boxwood all the way down
to Bellagio. And best of all,
one room remote and quiet
where he lay in the dark each morning
composing his thoughts.

There's a spider next to Pliny's
left knee, composing his web.
Pliny's nose is broken.
He sits in his carved robes
holding a book in his hand with one finger
missing, watching the lake.
He can barely see the view
from his little stone eyes,
for the scrub and the honeysuckle have grown wild
on the cliff before him.

The spider is doing what he knows best.
He spins from the knee to the hand of the statue
as if he were swinging on a kite string
across the whole sky. The late summer air
is thick with insects. It's a good life.
Even if it's somebody else's.

Stephen Berg

Oblivion

1

I thought the Greek root would tell me something I didn't know
but there is no Greek root—ME, MF, fr. L. oblivion-, oblivio
and then to forget, perhaps fr. ob- *in the way* + *levis* smooth—
an act or instance of forgetting... I thought it meant
        something like where we go
after death, i.e. "to oblivion," the future of us, the true,
inescapable condition of existence without consciousness,
human consciousness. So it's being forgotten more than anything
that hurts us, and immortality is—to be remembered?
What it really means is what someone said to me a few months ago
when I said, "I've always thought of you as immortal, I guess,
but now I know you're not." "Yes, I am. I'm in your mind," he
        replied.
It's that "in your mind" that has a kind of murderous
        tenderness,
it's like saying someone *let* himself be part of you, to help
        you, yes,
but also because he trusted he could not be destroyed by your
        mind,
just as a mother takes up a screaming baby into her arms
and croons to it and pats it over and over Now Now Now she
        whispers and presses
the helplessly small body to her breast and it
calms, whimpers, calms fully and falls asleep there.

2

The elephant-gray elms bathed in overcast light glow.
Cobalt-blue sky peeps through hills of shaggy clouds.
Windy and cold, 30 on the thermometer outside my window,
chirpings off to my right from behind Jim Wilson's house,

branches stripped clean, bouncing and waving, the day bright,
      brighter,
then darkening under speeding clouds, everything held,
accepted, in an order, the mind and world one
forgetting in which only this moment has meaning. It's much
      much clearer now.
All's changed color: the lime-freckled salmon brick of Jim's
      house,
for example, suddenly flares crimson, fists of ailanthus pods
and stuccoed housewalls seem the same bleached tan, even the
      copper cross,
(lived here ten years and I never noticed it) perched on the church
      tower
a block northeast is greener, complete because of the light.
But it's the jumble of stacked, rusting
tricycles and two-wheelers leaning against the side of a house
      on the backyard shed roof
and the oval yellow plastic wading pool tilted on edge
next to them and the cement bucket, white, left on the shed and,
      most, the homemade red
white and blue doghouse set down a few feet from the shed
that give this life its fullness, for now—
the innocent, peaked, green tarpaper roof and doorless door look
      kind,
a gift of absent hands, of animals taken in, fed.

Ben Belitt

Annunciation to Joseph

Looking up from the bole
on the ringleted carpenter's block,
the incense under the saw,
he paused as the blade buckled and the sunburst
opened an improbable fan in its blinding serrations.

And thought:
           All goes as it must.
A fragrance of resin and camphor sweetens the saw-horse.
The ruler's edge measures the place where the stylus
passed over, to a decimal fraction,
wedge matches wedge and confirms the plumb-line's vibration,
the part vanishes into the whole.
The reckoning is just.

Then how is it everything goes so abstract?
The blueprint trembles with musical signatures
and wherever the balancing bubble has lain,
an angel works in the grain,
the posts of the temple are moved (as the prophet has said)
and the saw's tooth snaps on the knot.

What should a sawyer's apprentice
know of the marvelous, or an angel require
of him? One beam weighs down another.
The roof rises over the inn and the stable,
the pedestal leaps from the plinth.
Shall the thing that is building rise on a palpable loss?
The journeyman has his reward, the builder is worthy his hire.

I am moved by no journeyman thing.
I smell dung on the terebinth
floor, and the ox's stall curves like a cradle.
The arches reject the seams of the pillar in their

103

Roman similitude, the ogives pull
to a point as if to outdistance creation
and gather all under their wing.

Something is building.
The consort of Solomon calls from the garden:
the godson awakes with the bridegroom
and the virgin lies down with the bride.
Shall they join what the axe and the hammer never hewed
out of cedar and granite?
Does the whole of the carpenter's subtlety end and begin
with a cross?

A carpenter's son does well to be wary.

Hail, Mary!

Allison Funk

Mirrors

1.

The last weeks she seemed lost in a wish
to be free of us, all the blossoming
and detritus. In her darkening room
she dreamed of a place unpreyed upon,
resistant as ice is to sun in the cliffs.
But we could not accept it,
we, the family who had given her a new heart,
brilliant cloak for survival. Like the birds
we went on forever, interrupting the night
with our familiar colors and songs.
At last miniature, her thirst
unbearable, she had no voice to *remember,*
though I held my newborn for her to touch,
the closest of us to the source.

2.

A life can find its way into so many
branches, into cinder, into the column
still standing. My grandmother
had a Japanese maple, its leaves
not exactly blood red. If my memory
has a color, it is the burnt purple of those leaves
as dark in April and June as in autumn.
I could say that the tree
always warned of the end, that beautiful tree
standing between the house and the road,
the house and the garden. But I resist
seeing those ragged leaves
as her hands failing, will deny
the flesh its symbol and ash.

3.

The dust is everywhere,
draping the roof, resting on fences.
Covered, the bushes have nearly merged:
one full-figured, the next in tow;
some with arms around one another.
I remember sleeping in her bed
under an oval frame. Inside
was a child so plump I wondered
at the weight the Madonna held.
My grandmother told me stories to sleep,
calling me daughter. If she could now
she would say the snow is a blessing
over the broken ground, so thick
are the stars not of our planting.

4.

The last day I wheeled her into the sunlight,
her feet with no will of their own
brushing the lawn. She could hardly speak,
so motioned she wanted to hold my son
in the shade. Remember your cherry tree,
I said, how each season
you hung the mirrors of aluminum on its branches.
Was it their image or the sound of metal
beating metal in the wind
that frightened the birds from your fruit?
Then I could not look into her face,
seeing the cardinals, the seeds
she scattered for them,
the cherries bent around their stones.

Roger Skillings

When No One Is Looking

Stow my foreign ashes in some rubble pile,
Crypt-cranny, chink or rodent hole
Amid some ancient crowded ossuary
Sun-whitened by the sea, in sound of hooting ships—
Nice, maybe, or Venice—some great ornate
Cypress-haunted shrine of fatalistic tombs,
Epitaphs pious, stoic, mocking or profane,
Pompous mausoleums, costly sarcophagi, statuary
Quick with lizards
                   Along formal well-kept paths
Where time-struck tourists may linger and stare,
Aware of the sharp-edged shadows, the protean dust,
Where surely once an age must come some
Merciful necromancer with news of history,
How fares the human race,
And whether sense has yet been found
Or an end of woes. And has death died?
And is there hope for us?

I was a New England atheist, b. 1937, inconsolably
curious about the cosmos, fearfully dubious of the
future of life, whose any arrant cell seemed grander
than all inanimate marvels, origins and ends great
or small, whatever the denials of nothing are
and anti-zeros too, cascading through inconceivable
kaleidoscopes of order, chaos or whatever else
may be, transient or not, redolent finally only
of ennui, with none to know, none to mull, none
to praise, endure, master or explore. Forever
my ego could not bear. Life was too short
in good health.
                  Disparate, chill, claustrophobic
in time, too proud to hope, too provincial to care
much for other possible beings, and quite sure

107

(despite a lifelong proclivity to err)
that few if any gods would turn up soon,
nor many powers to love be found beyond our own
brief selves and progeny, I nevertheless, like a sly
deathbedded convert taking no chances, do hereby
adjure my friends to let some certain trace of me,
glitter of bone-ore, ash-flake or cinder,
abide in some fecund storied place—Malta, say,
or Napoli, Corinth or old Thebes.
                                    In life I never
felt at home, bore neither kith nor kin in deepest
heart, chiefly struggle knew, discouragement, rage,
doubt, pride and secret fear, spent my mortal years
coffined in my brain, and wrote my works, more
mortal things for sure, but true runes of the vanished self,
a-mingle now, I trust, amongst the eon-avid atoms
of the warm Mediterranean. In vain I searched for a soul,
found only an egoistic agony of desire to doubt my end
                        but
all the same, just in case, lest I be lonely, unheeded, wrong,
leave some ignorant wishful speck of me in some famous
        sacred place,
and please, *mes amis,* save the libraries and graves.

And ever and anon, Hail, unique kindly one! Speak:
What's the age? What news? How go the wars with death?
How fares the human fate?

Lucie Brock-Broido

In a Landlocked Time

And there is nothing
like the mistral love of fishermen
devoting their days to the sea.
That is the kind of love
which I require
the forty years of worship
for the weather, the never ending days
of dawns, the homage to the
captured thing.

A year ago, I was preparing my body.
It was magical, a scouring,
the long oiled baths, the embalming
with fragrances and color, my long love
of ritual. When all else fails
you will see me resorting
to mythologies and I become
the Hyperborean girl
that I am.

As of yesterday, it was irrevocably
fall. There was to be no turning
back, we were deep into it then.
I am attendant
on this time the time
between the north wind
and the present tense.

The landlord had tied down the trees,
wrapping their roots in canvas cloths.
He put out offerings,
the bucketfuls of sand
left at the top and bottom
of each set of stairs.

109

Even the salt air could not undo
the ice.

He was preparing us
for storm. He was preparing
for a time when the lights would burn
even by day.

In our small town
by winter, when only the warmblooded
were left to spare each other
of the bitter cold,
it was only the fishermen
who could redeem us then.

Archimages of the shallow bay,
magicians even of the deepest sleep,
they could call out of hypnosis
the water-breathing creatures
which were slowing in the middle
of their tracks, their long descent
into a winter's night.

I am a creature
of the real world
even though you think
I seldom choose to live there properly.
I am an air-breathing
sort: always cold
at the extremity, never content
with the love that I have.

When my limbs were clean
and brand new and I wrapped you in
myself when we moved deeper
north, then there was no turning

back. That is the kind of language
I require,
the four seraphs of the wind, the

Holy holy
as they move in toward the land
where I live now.

A year ago
I was waterproofing myself in virgin wool
for the cold ride out
to watch the whales
as they waited for winter
and hesitated, not too far
from land. In a landlocked time

I have never seen their great
grey backs bending the surface
of the sea
never seen their cool reluctance
to stray too far from human warmth.

Poem for My Ten Thousandth Day

When everything seems a message
a small cue of light beneath the door,
shadows that move too early when the thing
which they are mimicking is still,
the car crash at Lochlyn
in the middle of the dawn
& no survivors anywhere in sight.

111

Not that I don't have the same chemicals
that everyone else has too.
It isn't that I am alone
or that my certain breed
of bliss catches fire in the wrong
times & I'm bewildered with a joy
so large that I would wish to die.

It comes down to this:
Tonight is my ten thousandth night.
It happens in the middle
of my twenty-seventh year.
I am one third done

with this. It happens suddenly
without warning, like the diabolical loss
of signal lanterns in electrical storm,
like a wound appearing out of nowhere
where before had been clean flesh.

I kept hearing about the Underground
in reckless cities all over the world,
how important danger will become in a tunnel
situation. How caution means nothing,
how the music of traveling
too fast has everything to do with risk
& melancholia. I am drawn
to figments & occasion:

REM sleep, Winter Solstice, the Blind Man's
afternoons. I would read for him
in an Oriental room which smelled of dread
& dance there for him barefoot
on a black rug, as if he could see
the color of the inside of my mouth
from a room six hundred miles away.

I have come to this.
Those of us whose eyes by chance,
genetics, aptitude, go down on the ends
will be perceived as perpetually sad.

There is nothing quite exact to fear
& these are hours of exactitude.
As if it would be possible to live
in random increments or know that no one
knows which thing will happen next.
This many days into my life
I have come to this:

December, I am in possession
of my name.
Sorcerer, this is substantial life
we're speaking of.
Light, you
loom upon these days
as if everything has its certain purpose
like an inebriated monk illuminating
a great text.

Olga Broumas

Perpetua

As the seed of a mole for
generations carried across
time on a woman's belly
flowers one morning blackly
exposed to poison and poison
itself is not
disease but mutation is one
understanding the strong
shaft of your clitoris I kiss
as the exposed tip of your
heart is another.

For Every Heart

I like it best when my friend has lovers, their happy moans,
unrestrained, fill the house with the glee of her prowess.
As in China during the concert of the laser harps
cameras added their applause, percussive
while the umbilical fanned neon from each note
in the open air theater and ribboned the path of stars,
I am moved to clap. Hands clapping calm us.
It is their simple, wholehearted and naive sexual imitation,
their fleshbird dance chest high in the open
of time.

After

Influenced by a great largesse which affected
our destinies we were abandoned as by charm

to the involuntary, light mammal lust and rasp,
like an ephemeral birthmark bared to the sun

on the still pink terrazzo between breasts.
The porch led to a drop, a hidden valley

whose opposite south slope slanted to sea.
Far to one side a low stone wall, donkeys

and butterflies in its keep, quiet enough
to hear our heart if not for birds in full

song and too dense to descend without a spiral
which was done with village stones. Words

are black where there are stars. I'll never
have a child you said one morning, I can't

remember when I made up my mind. Mind, child,
stone. The heat flattens and coats them. They turn

from black to white and whiter, air. The wind
blows them back into place again and the grass

heaves a little where we had lain.

Edward Field

Dedication

Away from home on a tour in the West
I worried about you constantly, my dearest,
until I had a dream one night where you
were a large plant I was chopping down with a shovel:
First I slashed off your feet
and then battered your head in, that head
that has already been attacked
by scalpel, drill, and saw,
and is always blindly bumping things,
making my heart ache.

I woke in a sweat of course
but after the shock wore away that I
could do such a thing to you, my angel, even in a dream,
I saw how absolutely necessary it was—
your needs had pursued me across a continent
and this was the only way of getting free, of renouncing
even for a week the relentless care of you,
the concern of my days and nights: How to keep you,
an exotic, delicate plant, alive in an arctic clime—
though in my dream, I must admit,
you were a vigorous weed, overtopping me.

And then, my leafy, my green one,
whom I water daily and put in the sun,
after chopping you down and shoveling you away
I could leave you in God's hands—
and loving you not the less for being free,
went almost lighthearted on with my journey.

Triad

A temple sculpture: Two warriors in combat,
down between their knees a female
with the prick of one of them up her cunt
and at the same time bending over backwards
to take the other's cock in her mouth—
while the men cross swords over her.

Even confronting each other with sharp steel,
according to this ancient mystery
something tender bridges them,
a goddess joining the warriors in her body—
for she has to be a goddess
and this is obviously her function.
But is she consoling, neutralizing,
trying to bring peace about?
Or delivering the charge that sets the swords a-clashing?

Or do they only appear to fight
to deny the sexual connection below?
But no one seems to be hiding anything—
it's open as a diagram, illustrative,
rather than a daisy chain like The Three Graces.

When we say men are joined in battle
do we too mean like this,
opposition at one pole, concord at the other,
and in the contest both at once?
Beyond the fierce worldly display,
the glitter of rivalry, the squiring of women—
a secret brotherhood?

And this goddess created out of mutual need
as if maleness cannot mate without a medium—
it's within a female principle men unite.

117

Myra Sklarew

At the Syrian Border

Walking between two mine fields
I pretend I am a tourist here: What trees,
I say. What mountains. I mouth
slogans bitter as a salt sea.

The wind feeds on the basalt rock.
Under every eucalyptus there is
the yawning shadow of a bunker. My people
is an armed camp.

I remember a boy who made a bridge
of his body for the others to climb across.
They turned him into air and fire and earth.
And here is the place where a father

let his child down a knotted sheet
like Jacob, only not going up.
One child by one child down the ladder
of knots and when he himself climbed

down for the last time he found each one
murdered. O Jacob let us put away
our strange gods. My people is an armed
camp. Her sons wear old faces.

Jason Shinder

Boat Knocking in the Wind

I say ocean and all I can think about
    are your green eyes.
Imagine: I don't know anything
    about you.
Only this: a studio with one window
    overlooking the bay
and you are here like a boat knocking
    in the wind.
Being a poet you may not like the simile.
    Especially these days
you probably think you're the wind.
    You're right.
You can be sure I do too. Sure you're the wind.
    And what's even more terrific?
You're also the flat sky and beach of this Cape
    and the green stone
I found yesterday and picked up for no reason.
    They're all the same thing:
loss. Only the one lying outside the heart
    is safe. You understand?
Anyway all this is talk. It's just more
    of our talk,
sleepless, irritable, bull-headed talk.
    It's all or nothing
I say, with a blind, good-for-nothing sadness
    for the look in your eyes
approaching desire, in which you forgot
    yourself, youthful
I could say the way your hair falls
    across your forehead
in the picture on the wall. I can't tell you
    how vivid this feeling is,
continuous as the waves, which I'm afraid
    will wash over everything

before I have another chance to sit with you
    on the bus and go shopping
in one of those boutiques where the owner
    tips his hat because
he knows us. Must I admit I chose
    this ending? If ever
I had something to say
    it should be now, but I can't
bring myself to say it
    or I forget. I'll just
listen to the waves divide
    among the stones.
I'll just listen to the boat knocking
    in the wind because
it blushingly pauses now
    and then
to remind me how once you were struggled for.

for K. W.

William Jay Smith

Gardens

For Stanley Kunitz, poet and gardener

"Now that is what I call a garden!" the reluctant Texan tourist
exclaimed to his wife. He gestured from the upper balcony
of Powis Castle, on the border between Wales and England,
toward a wealth of statuary, Italianate balustrades
and stairways, lush perennial borders, formal terraces
(each with its distinctive feature, the first, a line of yews
like a row of giant gnomes' hats hung along the walls)
spilling over with musk roses, wisteria and clematis
to a green park-like basin below
and the cloud-swept Shropshire hills off in the distance.

Your Cape Cod garden is a far more modest affair,
having all that a garden needs,
"plain bricks, wood, water, and plenty of plants,"
as that essential earthman, Henry Mitchell, would declare,
a place the color of earth and air,
that makes you feel, when you step into it,
that you have come out of a desert
and found, as if dreaming,
a Rousseau-like jungle, dripping and steaming,
where passion like the peony may have its province
and simple patience flower in the shade,
where daffodils flare back like mules' ears,
a place where one may sit and mull things over,
savoring, from the darkest depths, with your trumpeting vines,
your stiff grass spears,
your billowing trees,
a poet's lines,
reminding us that gardening, like the writing of poetry,
is among the most natural and rewarding—
and yet most mysterious—of human activities.

Östen Sjöstrand

X-ray Picture

He saw a park bench broken in two by a large rock. Not
completely in two, for the two halves still hung together.
He tried to bend them back, to fit the splintered parts
together again, and return the bench intact to its place
in the spruce grove. But it was as if the bench pursued an
inner resistance of its own. Reluctantly he withdrew across
the lawn—
   And the hammer is lifted against the Greek urn: the microfilms
of runways and mountain hangars is handed over at the secret
meeting place; the bed is made up again—and without a sound,
with a soft ball stuffed into his mouth, he falls flat on his
face in the hallway, pursued to the very end by a savage pack
of dogs he had once taught to hunt.

Translation by William Jay Smith and Leif Sjöberg

Memory Image

She held the little boy by the hand and led him toward me.
They were both naked, but the woman was wearing a strange
Phrygian silver cap. I was struck by how freely the child
moved, and how independent he seemed. (Outwardly he resembled
the young acrobat painted by Picasso.)
   Then, I thought, the terrible destructive planetary cloud
has not doomed me to be forever childless. But the boy's face
did not belong to me but to other parents.
   The woman, seeing that I was in a state of near exhaustion,
pointed at a mountain. Was she pointing to a tomb amid rocks,
meaning for me to make a pilgrimage to it? But I was so weary
that such a journey was possible only in thought.

122

But I stopped thinking about myself. And I saw at the same time that the rock was split through and that the boy had emerged from the rock: that he had been there from the beginning.

I got up from my chair, climbed the stair, extending my hand to her whom I loved from the depth of all time.
Together we strolled off to the kitchen. The day was not yet over.
And soon in the late dawn wind the night's shadows would

disperse.

Translation by William Jay Smith and Leif Sjöberg

B. H. Friedman

Tribute to a Survivor

About thirty years ago Stanley Kunitz walked into Abby's and my living room—and into our lives—escorting Dorothy Miller of the Museum of Modern Art to a spontaneous party after an art opening. When Stanley was introduced to me, I asked, "Are you the Kunitz of Kunitz and Haycraft?" referring to the editors of the biographical dictionary *Twentieth Century Authors.* He said he was, seemed offended, insisted on his identity as a poet.

Subsequently I read some of his early poetry but, for a while, continued to think of him as the editor of my often-used reference book and also as someone who, like many poets living in New York, moved in the art world and admired the scale and energy of contemporary American painting. In that world, too, I met the poet and painter Elise Asher. However, it was not until 1963, after Stanley and Elise were married and when Abby and I began spending summers on Cape Cod, that we got to know them well.

In New York there were plants in his home. In Provincetown he spent hours on the creation, under difficult conditions, of a glorious rock garden.

In New York there had been talk of tennis. In Provincetown he played—steadily and aggressively—sometimes leaving his regular doubles game to set up highly competitive matches between poets and prose writers or writers and artists. He hated to lose. He hated particularly for poets to lose. Perhaps no defeat was more bitter than a match he lost with Robert Lowell as his partner. Stanley seemed unable to believe that a poet as good as Lowell could play such bad tennis.

In New York he asked how my work was going. In Provincetown he read some of it, and he introduced me to other writers. When I mentioned my admiration for Allen Tate's novel *The Fathers,* Stanley produced the author—almost immediately, it seemed—at a small dinner party, a party that

124

began with an introduction as inauspicious as my own to Stanley. This time, Abby said to Tate, "Oh, I always see you at the liquor store."

In New York Stanley and I talked sometimes about drinking as an occupational hazard. In Provincetown we jointly celebrated our birthdays (July 27 and 29). During two decades, these parties enlarged and, with the founding of the Fine Arts Work Center, began to include more younger writers and artists. They appreciated Stanley's clam chowder seasoned with herbs from his garden and my dune-dry martinis.

In New York we went separately to the Strand and Gotham Book Mart. In Provincetown we made long excursions together to the huge Parnassus Book Store in Yarmouthport.

In New York we argued about *Moby-Dick,* one of my replies to Stanley's assertion that poetry was necessarily superior to prose. In Provincetown we went on whale watches and when we saw "Braid," a badly scarred survivor of a ship's propeller, we knew there was nothing to argue about. As much as the sea itself, this great arched creature was both poetry and prose, as Stanley demonstrated in his 1981 poem on a whale beached in Wellfleet.

In New York, especially when I first met Stanley, he spoke of T. S. Eliot as a god. In Provincetown, years later, he began to speak thus of William Carlos Williams and, still later, of Walt Whitman.

Yes, Stanley opened and expanded on the Cape, and so did his work. His poetic line became longer, freer, closer to natural speech. It's a joy to see anyone—but especially this generous man with such wide interests—still growing at eighty.

Daniel Halpern

Of Caravaggio

No man could paint such things who didn't know.

Caravaggio's dark sweeps up to brush
distinctly the white cloth of her shoulder.

She bends her head toward her knee, her cheeks blush
a pinkish light.

           At her fingers a string
of pearls, less trifle than serpent—she'll bring
back what she needs.

           Her pale hair holds the dark
at bay, her green dress, or jade, billows out
its small lime fire and at her throat her heart,
beating gently on the vein.

                She's aglow
within her light.
           Who is it behind her?

No man could paint such things who didn't know.

You see how he's established her posture,
allows her to reach for what she sees below.

She's turned away from what took place, demure—
his hand? something said?—her eyes refuse to say—
and behind her the artist's dark display.

He covets what he knows, what his hand draws pure.

Words of Advice

Language held you above the water,
you breathed,
you took hold of yourself.
Off the mill ponds, light
fired the discursive
opportunities of the scene.
You called back
pre-dark meals as a child
among those of your blood.
Write me
someone with years of stability
asked of you
as another year turned.
And what was it your mother told you
never to forget?
They've taken away your father
and the little song
you remember him by.
It goes like this. . . .

You called back the young women—
their slender, lonely bodies
stayed awhile at your side,
they said what they had to.
Make it easy on yourself,
there comes a time
when you'll sit down alone,
finished with yet another story,
and begin to assemble
what has been given over to you—
your face remembers

its repertoire of moves,
and there is a song
that keeps you awake.
A single detail of light
is dragged over the water.
You called back
something you were told
not long before your father's death.
It was a little kindly advice,
surviving on the body of its melody,
the lyrics long ago lost on you.

Things That Make the World Worth Saving: An Introduction to a Poetry Reading

Stanley Kunitz gets along well with animals. He once found a family of five owls out in the woods, and for six weeks stood under the nest for an hour each day. After a while, he says, "I could reach up and pet them. I remember touching one of the adult owls and discovering how tiny he was under all those feathers. Finally, I walked out of the woods one day with all five of them sitting on my shoulders."

This same patience and apparently endless energy to understand the new and unknown is given to the hundreds of young poets who have come to him as students, friends, seekers of advice and criticism. The experience of an afternoon at the Kunitz's with Stanley working over your poems is something no writer is likely to forget. Theodore Roethke, were he alive, would testify to this—he was one of the first young poets to come knocking on Stanley's door to discuss poetry.

Stanley's own literary recognition came early. It began in the fourth grade, when his teacher read aloud his essay entitled "The Father of Our Country." It began like this: "George Washington was a tall, petite, handsome man." Stanley says of this seemingly contradictory offering, "Of course, I had no idea what "petite" meant, but I loved the sound of it...." This love of sound, the sound of words, has never ceased—it has become the personal mark he has stamped on contemporary poetry. Since that fourth grade classroom, his poetry has won for him all the major honors that are occasionally bestowed upon the deserving. If one has an argument with his poetry, it's that there isn't enough of it. In sixty years of writing he has published some 200 poems—not an overwhelming amount. Stanley says, "Over a lifetime I've written poems only when I felt I had poems to write. I do not feel apologetic about refusing to convert myself into a machine for producing verse." This July he was 80—55 years since the publication of his first book, *Intellectual Things.* Although the book was well received, it was not until his *Selected Poems,* published in 1958, that he was appropriately recognized with the Pulitzer Prize.

In 1975 he was Poetry Consultant to the Library of Congress. And he was editor of the Yale Series of Younger Poets for six years, but unlike his predecessors, he refused to allow readers to filter the manuscripts that were submitted, which means each spring he enlarged his contact with young poets by another thousand or so manuscripts. He continues to read and help organize the new books of his many ex-students, as well as others who seek his help. He is one of a handful of older poets who is aware of what's being written around the country—he makes it a point to know, and he cares about it. And with all this, he continues his own work. He has just published a new collection entitled *Next-to-Last Things.*

It was my intention to make this a more personal note, to express what I feel about Stanley Kunitz, who was my teacher, and whom I've had the good fortune to see often during the past fifteen years. Our talks have always been various and unpredictable—from the art of waxing floors to a discussion regarding the textures of men's shirts—on this particular occasion, he brought down a pile of old shirts for a young poet who was also visiting, and asked her to try each one on. She left with three of them. And one Saturday in the mid-seventies we watched the Kentucky Derby together—he had a poet's intuition riding on Prince Thou Are—the prince came in sixth. However, in the ultimate order of things, this miscalculation isn't important. With the sure-fire acumen that earlier juxtaposed petite and tall, the poet's intuition chose resonance of language over the shallower glory of the winner's circle. Stanley is supremely informed, and there is very little that doesn't interest him. With the same expertise he calls forth in discussing poetry, he outlined, that Saturday after the race, the rules that govern the naming of race horses. No more than 13 letters. No more than three words. The name should somehow allude to the horse's genealogy.

It is important to understand the elements that come together to complete the poem in the man and to understand the things that for Stanley ultimately make the world worth saving: Kunitz the cook—his ten-ingredient soup. Kunitz the carpenter. Kunitz the horticulturist, the naturalist, the humanist—his belief in the sacredness of poetry. Stanley says, "I think of poetry partly as a game, partly as an ordeal, and I confess to ignorance of the boundaries. This is the danger of wordplay: that it may lead to revelations. The path to the true voice of feeling, as Keats called it, runs through a forest of lies. What do I really know except that I am living and dying at once? The taste of that knowledge on my tongue is that last secret I have to tell."

Peter Klappert

from *A Revolving Meditation for Stanley Kunitz*

Agh! I am sometimes weary
Of this everlasting search
For the drama in a nutshell,
The opera of the tragic sense,
Which I would gladly be rid of.
> —Stanley Kunitz, "Revolving Meditation"

4.

Two hours formulating a question for the *I-Ching*!

Paddling with a board
ripped from the useless pumphouse: Hard, and hard
on the fingers cramped around the pen.
Easier to tack, to point up into
the prevailing west, even in this old rowboat.

How much I disapprove of it!
How little I love it!

Easier to let the breeze carry me—

Not I, not I, but the wind
that blows through me

What kind of light did I expect?

Easier to zigzag
on the diagonal westward. Water lights
pattern the lake bottom. Water-striders,
long fronds of hornwort combed by a school of minnows.
Red-wings in the reeds. No way to J-stroke
with an old board.

Delta, marsh, hummock.
Bur-reeds and grasses.

Last year's
cattails like soft sculpture,
wind-blown and torn.

Why should I be bothered with it?

From this end of the lake
you can see the whole of Mount San Angelo.
The small cedars cone as if clipped,
the taller cedars spread and pyramid,
staggered up the hill among pines.
Trucks on 29 audible but hidden, the pastures
rise toward the mansion, all but
invisible in hemlock, spruce, and the vast,
domed crown of the copper beech.

The eye moves past
the elaborate important landscape
—an arboretum reverting to wilderness, but held—
past maple, elm and oak, linden, black walnut,
weeping cherry, redbud and Kentucky coffee-berry,
the eye reaches through ailanthus, dogwood and Paulonia
toward Bill and Juliana's house (a white splash
glimpsed in shades and levels of green)
and falls
forward and down to the one man-made color, blue-green,
the boathouse settling, its peak already folding
toward the lake.

Drifting now, the boat
going broadside, then turning bow to wind
on its skeg, stopping, and spinning the lake
shore back the other way,
                              swinging and
eddying each thing

                      calling me swings my attention
like a great round weight at the end of a cable
each thing a summons

                              the summons in the telephone
—parents, office, mechanic, student, lover—
the summons in the book I was reading
when the sunlight dimmed and went out and rain
came riding a black wind over the sill, the summons
at breakfast in the newspaper, too many summonses
to be in India or Paraguay, in London, Atlanta,
to go to the store, to appear at 9:30
at the Biograph, to see the paintings, to make
reservations, the summons at the door, through
the mailslot, through the open window across
the street and on the radio, the tiny summonses of
gnats falling at the base of my lamp and on my desk,
that summons, the letter calling to be read, reread,
and memorized,

                      each thing taking the brush
of my attention, each thing passive, obdurate,
implacable, wilting, dropping petals, chilling
my shoulders, each thing insistent, nothing complete
completed ready finished dead to me no journey
completely made no book read or written each thing
a summons

to answer to come back
to take up the board and head the boat
downwind to let it bear me
                                    carry me toward the shoreline
where the Holsteins now are walking, toward the two
lakeside tulip poplars that rise and split and rise again,
toward the world there, cow-eyed and dawdling
but—yes—coming down to the causeway dam to meet me.

Heidi Jon Schmidt

On Stanley, at Eighty

With the reach of a Giant Sequoia
Daedalian as the Dead Sea Scrolls,
If he sat on his haunches at Gizeh
Stanley couldn't be any more old.

He exudes his exuberant aura
As he waters hydrangea or rose,
A lord of Elysian flora
With live eyes and convolvular nose.

Our tutor of matters transcendent,
A truth-rooted, light-loving man,
He's branched in relentless ascendant;
Stones fill to fruits in his hands.

How lucky to know Mr. Kunitz!
The sage pinching bugs from his Sage
Who has given his heart to his students:
May he lend his green soul to the age.

Mark Rudman

Thursday, October 17:
Worcester, Massachusetts

On the last day of the week-long Stanley Kunitz Poetry
Festival a group of us went with Stanley and Elise to see
some of the places of his childhood—the house where Stan-
ley Kunitz was born, the house at 4 Woodford Street where
he lived from age five until he left for college, the Quinna-
poxet reservoir, and what remained of Buteau's farm. These
are the "places" where the primal drama in his poems is
staged. If I focus on the house at 4 Woodford Street and
the reservoir, it's because they had the most impact on me.

On this brilliant fall day nature was undergoing a seizure
of clarity: there was no end to what you could see through
the transparent distances but no place we could stand, no
height, that had an unobstructed view. The house at 4
Woodford Street was no longer the last house at the edge
of town beyond which once lay fields and ponds and farms.

The reservoir was surrounded by small trees that were
still turning, fringed with yellow, though mostly gone to-
ward the red. It seemed much vaster than I would have
imagined from the poems, where he describes it, in "Quin-
napoxet" and "The Testing Tree," as "abandoned." And as
vast and wide and deep as it is unpeopled.

On reflection, this distortion, this reduction of matter to
its essential components, is at the core of his art and gives
his poetry the quality of being both specific *and* visionary.
The splendid isolation of each word in his work mirrors
the only (and "abandoned") child's dilemma in the world,
for it is only he who populates, who peoples this emptiness,
and who will so lovingly render the face of the father he
never knew in so many guises. He's always alert to the
doubleness of things that blaze in the "flash of recognition,"
as when he hears the "treetops seething" when the "sun
hung its terrible coals/over Buteau's farm," where he had
been "farmed out" as a boy.

The house at 4 Woodford Street was a grayish pink stucco. We stood in front of the imposing steps leading to its front door and I asked Stanley if he wanted to go in. We could always ring the doorbell! He said no, yet we remained standing, as if transfixed, in front of the stairs. At that moment the new owners arrived, carrying shopping bags, wearing blue jeans, the man sporting a kind of punk haircut. It was like a scene out of Robert Altman's *Nashville:* the group from out of town pulls up to the house as the new owners arrive at their own door, as if in expectation of the encounter, not only knowing who Stanley is but remembering articles in newspapers over the years and would have contacted him but didn't, thinking it would have been "too forward." They invited us in. Having come so far we could not turn back. (When the "Moon is at the door" it doesn't want to be asked in for "tea and comfortable advice.")

But there is a price to be paid for seeking. Stanley's cheek is still burning from the wordless slap he received from his mother for finding his father's portrait in the attic where he heard it thumping and bringing it down the stairs, on a kind of child's rescue mission, back into the light of day. I think of this burning as another form of fire stolen from the gods...which he has always transformed into energy.

The inner space of the house seemed to expand as we walked forward; it took on an expressionistic tilt. Rooms seemed to grow out of rooms, which is part of the design (was this his mother's intention?), so that it made me think of secret rooms, pantries and attics, more than living room, kitchen, bedroom. Or was it we who were deepening in the rooms? The new owners had all of their utensils and plants hanging from the ceilings: the house was their life! The wood had soaked up so much care. There was no question but that it was inhabited (and not merely by the—wonderful—new tenants). Stairs, doors, lintels, knots, enclosures, expanses, gardens—they were all there, more like characters in a tragedy than inanimate objects. A tragedy whose hero learned to see without sacrificing his sight. Gripped by emotions that threatened to reduce us to silence and quiet contemplation, we confined our response to questions about the house, both out of interest and as a way of staving off an undercurrent from becoming an undertow, the past from sucking us back.... Stanley pacing the garden ("my first garden," he said softly), surveying the sides of the house and the gutters and remembering the bird-feeder he installed, which was still there. The new tenants are restoring the house to remove the ghosts. We didn't go up to the attic.

Kenneth Koch

Letter

Stanley Kunitz, my wife Janice, and I wrote this poem one evening in Paris in 1954. I believe we took turns writing lines, and I think, but I'm not at all sure, that Stanley was the author of lines 1 and 4 of each of the first 6 stanzas and of the first half of line one and the second half of line two in the last stanza. In this same period, we were thinking about alternative versions of *Hamlet;* two I remember were a *Hamlet* with unchanged text but with all the characters on rollerskates, and another in which everyone was always smoking. Stanley and I had met for the first time a month or two earlier, at the old Opéra Comique, introduced by Jean Garrigue, whom I had met years before when I was in the army and she was a clerk in Sam Abramson's bookstore where I went to find books by Henry Miller. After this first meeting, Stanley and I saw each other often. He was very funny and smart and modest and also extremely eloquent on the subject of bad poets and their poetry. I loved to talk to him. He came to dinner at our tiny apartment on rue Notre-Dame-des-Champs. He himself was living in a *Quartier Latin* hotel with small rooms and a bedbug problem. Stanley read my poems. To my surprise, he liked some of them. I was surprised because I didn't expect anyone outside my group of painter and poet friends in New York to like what I wrote—especially not another poet. The attention he gave my work was exhilarating; he also often had ideas for making it better. Having all that intelligence and gaiety and perceptiveness that Stanley offered, being friends in the concentrated way one can be in a foreign city, was a great treat. It meant a lot to me. To Janice, too. The poem we three wrote seemed to me appropriate for this book not because it's one of Stanley's best works but because it is, for me, anyway, so full of the silly and literary happiness of our friendship then, when I was thirty years old and Stanley must have been fifty if he is about to be eighty now, both numbers seem a little surprising. Stanley, happy birthday!

Kenneth Koch

Another Perfect Day in a Fuzz Stampede

"Bastinadoes of rubbery elephants
Tear eternally through the fuzz
Toward Christmas, or Valentine's Day
Without the benefit of sassafras tonic"—
Then the coach began to speak less of Hinduism,
"Boys, keep your eye on the egg."

But the homunculus couched in that egg
And the comfortable charm of the elephants.
"In my day, there was too much Hinduism
Before our Sanskrit charms grew fuzz,"
He said, and rapidly drank a beaker of tooth-tonic.
6–0! The crowd went wild! "A love match!" Another perfect day!

There were flowers bubbling night and day
Where we children could see it, on the uppermost side of the egg;
We and none of our chums needed a tonic
To fall in love with our sloe-eyed elephants.
Anne said, "Joe, it's a night of gala fuzz!
Let's all go Hinduism!"

The Paraclete sang nine innings of Hinduism,
Thirteen of feathers, three of glue, and eight of day.
Then Stanley walked in, and frowned, "Oh fuzz!"
Till his grandmother rolled up in her chariot egg.
She startled the pin-striped elephants:
"Enough of this. Six days of sassafras and six of tonic!"

"Oh tell me! Are the fleas drunk on their elbow-tonic?"
"I put on the flannels of Hinduism."
O tigers! O hunters, Bengal, love! O gaudy, gauzy elephants!
Trumpets of umbilical day!
O Seasons! Why must you stomp on this glass egg?
He mumbled, as to strangers, through the darkening fuzz.

We are all vagrants, loving tender fuzz,
Loving the cast-iron appearance of tonic.
"I am your friend." (He strips off his disguise of ochre flannel.)
                    "Know me for the Egg."
And the egg's hatched within the egg of Hinduism!
Yes, it is! And on this nice yellow day
We're all standing here waiting for the elephants.

Bray, Pray! elephants! Easy goes the fuzz.
Down with day! A Ganges tonic
Formed me for Hinduism, who was once an egg.

Janice Koch
Kenneth Koch
Stanley Kunitz

141

Keith Althaus

The Garden by the Sea
To Stanley Kunitz

The gate swings in
on nerve noise,
rust, bees
in the salt air
moving the flowers
like a wind.
The real wind
at night,
off the Atlantic,
blowing pollen
and scents into the bay,
laying dust on the dark crests
of the waves.

Five different kinds of groundcover,
leaves I can't name, already dead,
floating back,
dropping in circles over the roots
that fed them.
The free-fall in the dark.
Rock willow, rock, sea ash.
The torpedo rush of air
like the surf roaring at night,
the stun of the breakers on your head.

Who ever heard of jasmine in Massachusetts?
Or of a rose bush that would save its last bloom
for the day you left for the city, no matter
how late you stayed into autumn? Surviving
all the early frosts, then dying quickly,
the next day, its petals dropping
as it knocked on the window of the empty house.
Who can find your door without amazement?

Roger Skillings

Early Days at the Fine Arts Work Center[1]

Of the founders, Stanley Kunitz had the largest, steadiest vision of the Fine Arts Work Center and what it ought to be. He fought hard for it, especially during the long birth throes, when everything was always in question and the future was threatened by an endemic parochialism. Often lonely, adept at committee steering, with many helpful friends in the worlds of poetry and art, he never spoke a word of despair or doubt, always knew the way was upwards, despite frequent contrary appearances and the skepticism of outsiders. He was the most eloquent, the surest and wiliest, the most respected and fearless, the strongest. He had the widest experience and deepest optimism, and his spirit impregnated the place.

It was the start of my green years. I retain a clear impression of the poet the day we new Fellows met him at the old rented Work Center on the corner of Standish and Bradford in November 1969, his motionless uninterpretable eye and somber hawk's head. To me he seemed old, old, yet some element of age was missing. He had a sort of simian bend and spider's hands, an inconspicuous grace that came—as I slowly learned—of the fitness and pride of a life of poetry, and one thing to him proved very like another in that all were done well, all with easy élan. He always seemed to have his whole being engrossed in whatever he was doing. He could stand in his garden in perfect stillness, knowing exactly where the paired garter snakes twined in his tri-peaked Alberta blue spruce. He wielded an infallible cure for the hiccups, as Mary Oliver will attest. He could cook up delectables with his own herbs, or hit a ball or throw a dart. Having survived fantastic Odyssean adventures in

---

[1] An arts community in Provincetown, Massachusetts, that grants fellowships to young artists, writers and poets.

143

youth, he won battles with the heart, the knife and the back, and mastered pain. He went on the road with his martinis in a jar, made a ritual of the husbandry he had learned from withdrawal. He once said that he might have been a kinder man if he had had something like the Work Center when he was our age, but I wondered if it was not the solitary ferocity with which he had beaten out the exile of his early years that had made his kindness so strong, so indifferent to any interest of his own.

His exultance at life seemed only to increase. He grew younger every year. Alan Dugan, no mean colloquist himself, said, "Stanley never gets tired of talking about poetry, he'll talk all night if you want."

After a reading at the Work Center he was apt to say, "Wellll...," calling out the word till it filled up with measured promise, "come back to my house and we'll have a nightcap."

A nightcap! What exhilarations were stored in the bottles at his house! An hour, two hours, three whirled by at the first of these séances, which always took place in his living room window, at the low round table with a pile of new books, often inscribed, the latest *Antaeus*, a basket of transcendent earth-and-sea-colored Shem and Shaun stones and a four-inch tarnished brass fly.

Eventually the brilliant glare of clarity stunned us all. Tom Lindsay, after a mad sly rant, had gone to sleep on the rug. Keith Althaus rolled on the gold antique sofa in an ecstasy of extreme notions and I was completely paralyzed. The silence lengthened into revelation. "How young you all seem!" he cried.

"Oh, Stanley," Jennifer Humphrey yelled with equal awe, "I've never seen people so drunk!"

"Ohhh," he said, flicking a hand, "I've seen drunker than this," and getting up to fill our glasses he fell onto the table.

But that story is one of a kind, and the truth is he tripped. Ordinarily he drank like Socrates, outlasted all the company, and lost neither his wits nor the next day, a useful knack in Provincetown.

As Jim Forsberg said, "If there's one thing we know how to do, it's throw a party." One couldn't not go—they were too good to miss, too many and too restless, I complained. "I know," Stanley said, "There's never anything to do but have another drink."

I remember one of B.H. and Abby Friedman's elegant evenings. Dinner done, some of the guests had formed a circle for further libations and the free exercise of their genius. Baxter Hathaway said Tolstoi was greatly overrated, absolutely a pedestrian bore most of the time. Myron Stout urbanely egged him on. The talk got uproarious, the jibes facetious, the critic more obstinate, crotchety and entrenched, while around the edges swirled an ebullient concatenation of fleeting controversies, calling up like nebulae the fabulous immortal names.

It was the height of summer, when the light stays and stays. In the shadowy room the ring of men had begun to bow and sway like behemoths, waving their arms. Stanley took his part but one eye was always out the broad window on the water, and finally I discovered, embedded in the dusk, inching home across the bay, a little orange sail.

He traveled widely, seemed to know every poet in America, especially the young, and knew writers everywhere, had read them all, living and dead, the whole tribe. In the Common Room at the Work Center, after a communal dinner, he described an International Poetry Festival in Rotterdam where he had talked with the Egyptian poet Salah Abdul Sabour about Palestine. He said, "We could have worked it out. We didn't always agree, but we could have worked it out. I know we could have. Of course you have to have some sense of the problem, some feeling for all sides."

His voice rarely lacked fire or carry, and to me at least, standing around with my Styrofoam cup of Cribari, it did not seem fantastic that the human fate hinged on such powers, that perhaps Plato had got it backwards in banishing poets and elevating philosophers to the ideal rule.

In February 1972 the Work Center had its second Annual Winter Blowup. The issues comprised a volatile stew of circumstance and misadventure and had simmered a good while, spreading strife at a time when all authority seemed an enemy.

A meeting was called and Stanley came up from New York. He sat in the back of the room on a window ledge while the ignorant brickbats flew along with fair comment.

Discontents of all sorts coalesced and a Jekyll & Hyde nest of hornets seemed to have materialized. One disgruntled young man said that "Stanley and his rich National Endowment friends could take their Fellowships and shove them."

Stanley rose to concede imperfection of the infant community, defend principle. Little by little it began to emerge that no malice was intended on anyone's part, that there were explanations and potentials if no immediate solutions, and that the Fellows too were responsible for making things work.

More grumbling was followed finally by Jennifer Humphrey intrepidly saying she thought the Work Center was a wonderful thing, after which a grudging silence lengthened out while the timid affirmers with prickling faces looked at the floor.

The most rebellious one persisted, sounding more plaintive, and expressed once and for all an everlasting characteristic, if not fault, of the Fine Arts Work Center, even down unto our own day: he said one's ego was always getting hurt.

With measured outrage Stanley said that in his experience life was a continuous assault on the ego.

Another silence set in, with nods. All had their say, and the end devolved in mollified feelings and general vindication. Time and again Stanley's presence dispelled smallness, meanness, falsity. He was like a gyroscope among people's better natures. He infused valor, inspired forthrightness and tolerance, provoked harmony, always invoked the common good, "and even, if one dare speak the word, a bit of joy!"

His rare anger was a moral indignation empty of any threat beyond itself. He never played the tyrant, even of the benevolent kind, and resigned many lost policy battles, suffered hard defeats and bled, but he had the necessary stamina to last, and was nearly the equal in equanimity of the imperturbable President and Chairman of the Board, Hudson D. Walker, who kept the faith and footed the bill in those early disastrous years of struggle to survive.

In August of '75 Gregory Corso, who happened to be in town, gave a reading in the bins at the new Work Center, originally Days Coal & Lumber Yard, 24 Pearl Street, renamed Joe Oliver Place, to honor the last owner, who wanted to assure artists the use of the studios forever.

It was a balmy night. The summer throng poured in. High overhead in the massive beams the dauntless swallows swooped to feed their ravenous chicks. It was the biggest crowd a Fine Arts Work Center event had ever drawn—surpassing even the balloon ascension of Brian Bolland—300 or so for the Beat Poet.

The next night Stanley read to about 50 in the gallery. "It hurts my pride," he said, driving out of the deserted parking lot. Keith and I stood there, shaking our heads, thinking our thoughts.

But Stanley gave the greatest reading I have ever seen. On the night of April 7, 1979, to a packed familiar audience overflowed into the office and spilled out of sight behind the gallery partition, standing around the walls, sitting on the floor in the corners back of the podium, he read only requests, and never had to wait for a flurry to choose from, never had to pick a single poem himself. From first to last the cherished names were called up without hesitation and were somehow apt in sequence, instinctive and shapely for the hour, ending with the triumphant and grievous incantation, "King of the River."

The ovation grew, held steady, dense, long. He came out into the office, bowed, fiery-faced, and the applause beat on and on.

And then there was wine in the Common Room, our after-a-reading ritual, and this one lasted long and late, and the excited genius of the gathered company was greatly on display.

I would praise the whole life, the entire being, the patiently sought inner music, his self-containment and Confucian self-mastery, his eternal rightness. He is a friend's friend, always full of news of friends, and he does not fail to censure when he thinks you are wrong. He is the wizard with his precious stones, his alphabet of secret cries, and his tribe of true affections, favorer of the maverick, fierce with his wry laugh of high irrepressible glee like a racehorse's whinny, tireless Battery Charger Supreme! Sublime! Ne Plus Ultra!

I do not know, over the years, how many have taken heart from the saga of his constantly growing younger and greater, more decisive, sagacious and clear, year on year, nor how many books he has inspired to enrich the world, but it must be many and many indeed, and we who love, honor and much owe him, are grateful on this occasion to celebrate the place and date, Worcester, Massachusetts, July 29, 1905, and are happy to say, "Happy Birthday, Stanley! More! More!"

Jack Gilbert

April Fool's Day on the Bus Going from Pittsburgh to New York

It makes me happy to write something celebrating Stanley Kunitz on his eightieth birthday. I know many people will honor him, as I have during the third of a century since the middle Fifties. But I would like also to thank him. Not just for the occasional kindness he has done me over the years, but even more for what he has been and is now. When I was a youth in the medieval city Pittsburgh was just before the Second World War, I dreamed of a civilization that lived just out of sight over the horizon four hundred miles away in Manhattan. A place where fine women read Proust in French and where my heroes, the writers, lived. Hemingway and Ezra Pound, Hart Crane and Thomas Mann, e. e. cummings and the crazy men Joyce and Faulkner. Where they lived at the same time they lived in Paris. As Thomas Wolfe (the real Tom Wolfe) lived there and simultaneously never left the rural small town North Carolina of my mother. As Hemingway lived in Italy and Spain and Africa and New York evidently all at the same time and fished them unceasingly. It was hard to be sure of whoever the man was that wrote the old black book titled *Personae,* which I'd stumbled across in a junk store, because every English teacher in Peabody High School said they had never heard of him. But I loved him and so decided he was in New York with the others who Scribner's published and the company that put pictures of a dog on their spine. A place impossibly far away to a kid in former Pittsburgh. (When I was a junior in high school, I discovered one of my best friends had never been even downtown.)

Eventually, I escaped and lived in Manhattan and Paris, and was a little famous and got to meet the really famous poets, and discovered that some were not like the great men I imagined them to be. So it mattered a lot to me when I met Stanley Kunitz and, later, George Oppen and Hayden

Carruth. Not that I can claim to be a close friend of any of the three, nor even to know them well; but it is true nevertheless. Doctor Johnson said no man should write the biography of a person he hasn't at least seen walking down the street. I have seen Mr. Kunitz that much and even a little more. I know. Just as I know from his poetry. I am grateful for what I have found there.

Year after year I have come across him. When I first lived in San Francisco and a hand of pinochle began to go against me, Jean McLean would start chanting happily:

Time swings her burning hands
I saw him going down
Into those mythic lands
Bearing his selfhood's gold,
A last heroic speck
Of matter in his mind
That ecstasy could not crack
Nor metaphysics grind.
I saw him going down
Veridical with bane . . .

And late at night on a rough Greek island struggling to carry the very heavy iron cylinder of butane across the stony fields in the starlight. Donald Brees, carrying the other end, saying out of nowhere: "Mobility—and damn the cost." Or the many times in workshops when I've explained the difference between simile and metaphor by quoting: "The night nailed like an orange to my brow."

Tony Bove explained to the teacher at *his* Pittsburgh high school (when she said to write a poem as the homework assignment) that it was impossible because he came from a family of Italian stone cutters. A couple of years later he learned to do it by reciting over and over and over:

In the zero of the night, in the lipping hour,
Skin-time, knocking-time, when the heart is pearled
And the moon squanders its uranian gold,

She taunted me, who was all music's tongue,
Philosophy's and wildernesses breed,
Of shifting shape, half jungle-cat, half-dancer,
Night's woman-petaled, lion-scented rose...

Was still reciting it when he came to visit me in Perugia. (Returned to Madrid where he was a professor and died a month later almost incidentally at the beginning of an important career as a poet.)

I think of taking Ginsberg to meet him when *Howl* was first popular. Allen began his dance about academics and Kunitz said, firmly, "Don't start that with me. I never wrote a sonnet in my life!" After which they had a good time together.

Recently in Florida I was in front of a television that was tuned to one of those mysterious channels that continuously transmit text. It may have been a cable schedule or market reports. I was doing something else when I heard that beautiful, silvery Kunitz voice coming out of the print. Saying, "Style has no virtue unless it lets you say what you want to say." And "The poet is the witness of what he has known." And:

I'm not a success. Never will be. And I don't want to
be... If you have chosen to be a poet, you have chosen
not to be a success. Success in poetry is almost a secret
to the mass of the population. The only success that
means anything is your own appraisal of yourself.

(Me running around like Cocteau's Orpheus trying to find a pen to get down what I had heard while listening to what was still coming out of the stolen car radio in his garage.)

Yesterday at the conference in Pittsburgh to celebrate 1985 as The Year of the Pennsylvania Writer, five novelists were going on about the mendacity of publishers and editors and critics and how you had to demand that any printing of your novel had to be more than 5000 copies or you were wasting your time (all of which may have been true for all

151

I know). After an hour of it, a young woman writer got up and quietly asked them to say something about style, and everything changed for almost ten minutes. It made me think of the piece I should be writing for the eightieth birthday of Kunitz and couldn't because I had committed myself to being there.

Earlier today I was on a panel of poets with Gerald Stern. He and I were trying to make the case for poetry being more than pleasure, more than making people feel good about themselves, and even more important than poetry as elegant tap-dancing. That it augmented civilization. Was a way of making the best we have known freshly alive inside the reader. Suddenly I thought of Kunitz asking himself in *The Thief* why he was there in Italy, and his answer:

> Some thirty years ago
> A set of lantern slides I saw at school
> Of these antiquities gave me an image
> Of the rare serene

Poems can make the largeness of the spirit and the ambitiousness of the heart manifest in us. In the same way, it is like that luminous beauty in the dark when I think of Stanley Kunitz: the loveliness in him, the courtesy of his mind, the grace of his spirit, his lyric seriousness, his *virtu*, his effortless intelligence.

I remember he said, when he was living in Seattle while he taught Roethke's class, that he could drive me any place in the city I wanted to go, but I had to take him to one of four places to begin. For years I deliberately misused this as a koan, puzzling over it without success. I think now that Stanley Kunitz in his poetry and in his being is one of the important places we can start from in order to get to where we should be going.

Acknowledgments

Cover photograph of Stanley Kunitz and photograph of Robert Motherwell's "Poet and Blank Page" by Renate Ponsold.

Photograph of Philip Guston's "Portrait of Stanley Kunitz" by Rudy Burckhardt.

Peter Balakian: "Clamming at Monmoy" is reprinted from *The Literary Review.* Copyright © 1981 by Peter Balakian.

Christopher Busa: "Stanley Kunitz: A Poet in His Garden" is reprinted from *Garden Design,* (Winter 1984–85). Copyright © 1985 by Christopher Busa.

Peter Davison: "The Winner" and "Crossing the Void" are reprinted from *The Atlantic Monthly.* "The Winner" copyright © 1958, 1974 by Peter Davison. "Crossing the Void" copyright © 1984 by Peter Davison. "Sperm and Egg" copyright © 1986 by Peter Davison.

Alan Dugan: "On Flowers, On Negative Evolution" copyright © 1985 by Alan Dugan.

Martha Friedberg: "Finally" is reprinted from *Choice.* Copyright © 1978 by Martha Friedberg. "Father" is reprinted from *Woman Poet.* Copyright © 1985 by Martha Friedberg.

Marie Howe: "Death, the Last Visit" is reprinted from *The Atlantic Monthly,* June 1984. Copyright © 1984 by Marie Howe.

Galway Kinnell: "Driftwood from a Ship" is reprinted from *The Past* published by Houghton Mifflin. Copyright © 1985 by Galway Kinnell.

Susan Mitchell: "The Falls at Otter Creek" is reprinted from the Poetry Society of America's *75th Annual Awards Ceremony.* Copyright © 1985 by Susan Mitchell. "Dirt" is reprinted from *Ironweed* and *New American Poets of the 80's* published by Wampeter Press. Its original title was "Boone." Copyright © 1984 by Susan Mitchell.

Mary Oliver: "Stanley Kunitz" is reprinted from the *Memphis State Review,* Fall 1984. Copyright © 1984 by Mary Oliver.

Linda Pastan: "Ethics" is reprinted from *Waiting for My Life*, published by W. W. Norton. Copyright © 1982 by Linda Pastan.

Robert Pinsky: "The Superb Lily" is reprinted from *Antaeus*. Copyright © 1985 by Robert Pinsky.

Michael Ryan: "My Dream by Henry James" is reprinted from *The New Yorker*, August 22, 1983. Copyright © 1983 by Michael Ryan.

Hugh Seidman: "The Great Ego of the Words" copyright © 1985 by Hugh Seidman.

Myra Sklarew: "At the Syrian Border" is reprinted from the *Reconstructionist*. Copyright © 1985 by Myra Sklarew.

Tom Sleigh: "Jenny Fish" is reprinted from *After One* published by Houghton Mifflin. Copyright © 1983 by Tom Sleigh.

Bruce Smith: "Silver and Information," "One Note Rage Can Understand," and "Snow on the Ocean" are reprinted from *Silver and Information*, published by University of Georgia Press. Copyright © 1985 by Bruce Smith.

May Swenson: "Morning at Point Dume" is reprinted from *Beyond Baroque*, Venice CA. Copyright © 1979 by May Swenson.

Ellen Bryant Voigt: "The Last Class" is reprinted from *Triquarterly* 58 (Fall 1983). Copyright © 1983 by Ellen Bryant Voigt.

C. K. Williams: "The Part" is reprinted from *Tri-Quarterly*. Copyright © 1986 by C. K. Williams.

Notes on Contributors

Elise Asher is a visual artist who has also published a book of poems entitled *The Meandering Absolute*. She is currently painting her own versions of "The Long Boat," a recent poem by Stanley Kunitz.

Dore Ashton has written eighteen books mostly about the visual arts.

Keith Althaus was a Fine Arts Work Center fellow and has been on the Writing Committee since 1973.

Yehuda Amichai's latest collection of poems is *Travels* (Sheep Meadow, 1986). His *Selected Poems* have recently been published by Harper & Row.

Peter Balakian's latest book of poetry is *Sad Days of Light* (Sheep Meadow, 1983).

Ben Belitt's new book, *Possessions: New and Selected Poems (1938–1985)*, will be published by Godine in the spring.

Stephen Berg's book of poems, *In It,* was published this spring by the University of Illinois Press.

Bohdan Boychuk is the author of six books of poetry in Ukrainian and is the editor of *Sucanist*.

Lucie Brock-Broido, a former Fine Arts Work Center fellow, has published poems in *Ironweed, Antioch Review, Southern Review, Ploughshares* and other publications.

Olga Broumas' first book of poetry, *Beginning with O,* was selected by Stanley Kunitz as the Yale Younger Poets Award for 1977.

Christopher Busa is co-editor of *Provincetown Arts* and recently interviewed Stanley Kunitz for the *Paris Review.*

Peter Davison's *Praying Wrong: New and Selected Poems, 1957–84* was published by Atheneum.

Alan Dugan recently published his *New and Collected Poems: 1961–1983* (Ecco, 1983).

Martha Friedberg has published two chapbooks, *Finally* (Vixen Press, 1981) and *The Water Poem and Others* (Vixen, 1985). She is co-founder of the Poetry Center in Chicago.

B. H. Friedman's most recent book, *Coming Close,* appeared in 1982.

155

Edward Field has published four books of poetry.

Allison Funk studied with Stanley Kunitz at Columbia University's Writing program in 1977. Her first book of poems, *Forms of Conversion,* will be published by Alice James Books next fall.

Tess Gallagher's *A Concert of Tenses: Essays on Poetry* will be published by the University of Michigan Press in the Poets on Poetry series.

Jack Gilbert recently published *Monolithos: Poems Nineteen Sixty-Two and Nineteen Eighty-Two* (Graywolf, 1984).

Louise Glück's most recent book of poetry is *The Triumph of Achilles* (Ecco, 1985).

Arthur Gregor is the author of eight volumes of poems including *Embodiment and Other Poems* (Sheep Meadow, 1982) and a memoir, *A Longing in the Land* (Schocken Books, 1983).

Daniel Halpern's most recent collection of poetry, *Seasonal Rights,* was published by Viking in 1982.

Robert Hass recently published a collection of essays entitled *Twentieth Century Pleasures* (Ecco, 1984).

Marie Howe studied with Stanley Kunitz at Columbia University's Writing Program in 1983. She has published poems in *Poetry, The Atlantic, Ploughshares* and *The American Poetry Review.*

Cynthia Huntington's first book of poems, *The Fish-Wife,* was published this spring by The University of Hawaii Press.

David Ignatow's most recent book is *Leaving the Door Open* (Sheep Meadow, 1984). His collected poems will be published by Wesleyan this year.

Shirley Kaufman's latest book of poems is *Claims* (Sheep Meadow, 1984).

Peter Klappert's *The Idiot Princess of the Last Dynasty* (Knopf) and *Fifty-Two Pick Up* (Orchises) appeared in 1984.

Galway Kinnell's most recent collection of poetry, *The Past,* was published by Houghton Mifflin in 1985.

Kenneth Koch's most recent books of poetry are *Selected Poems*

(Random House, 1985) and *On the Edge* (Viking, 1986).

Maxine Kumin's most recent collection of poetry is *The Microscope* (Harcourt Brace Jovanovich, 1984).

Cleopatra Mathis is a former fellow at the Fine Arts Work Center. Her most recent collection of poems is *The Bottom Land* (Sheep Meadow, 1983).

W. S. Merwin's *Opening the Hand* was published by Atheneum in 1983.

Susan Mitchell's poem, "The Falls at Otter Creek," won the Gertrude B. Clayton Memorial Award for a poem on the American scene (1984).

Hilda Morley's *To Hold in My Hand: Selected Poems 1955–83* was published by Sheep Meadow Press in 1983.

Stanley Moss will publish a new book in the fall.

Joyce Carol Oates recently published *New and Selected Poems 1970–1982* (Ontario). Her latest novel is *Marya* (Dutton).

Mary Oliver's third collection of poems, *Dream Work*, was published by the Atlantic Monthly Press this spring. She is on the writing committee at the Fine Arts Work Center.

Gregory Orr is the author of *Stanley Kunitz: An Introduction to the Poetry* (Columbia University, 1985).

Linda Pastan's sixth book of poems, *A Fraction of Darkness*, was published by Norton in 1985.

Robert Pinsky's most recent poetry collection is *History of My Heart* (Ecco, 1985). He has been a visiting poet at the Fine Arts Work Center.

Mark Rudman's book *In The Neighboring Cell* was published by Spuyten Duyvil in 1982.

Michael Ryan's second collection of poetry, *In Winter*, was published by Holt Rinehart & Winston in 1982.

Heidi Jon Schmidt will be Chairman of the Writing Committee at the Fine Arts Work Center beginning in the fall.

157

Grace Schulman's new study of *Marianne Moore: The Poetry of Engagement* will be published this year by the University of Illinois Press.

Hugh Seidman's most recent book, *Throne, Falcon, Eye*, was published by Random House in 1982.

Jason Shinder recently edited *Divided Light: Father & Son Poems—A Twentieth Century American Anthology* (Sheep Meadow, 1983).

Leif Sjöberg translated with Muriel Rukeyser *A Mölna Elegy* by Gunnar Ekelöf (Unicorn, 1984). Harry Martinson's *Wild Bouquet-Nature Poems* translated by William Jay Smith and Leif Sjöberg will appear in the spring (BkMk Press).

Östen Sjöstrand is a Swedish poet and translator. A member of the Swedish Academy, he is editor of the review *Artes*.

Myra Sklarew has most recently published two books of poetry, *The Science of Goodbyes* and *The Travels of the Itinerant Freda Aharon*.

Rose Slivka, Chief Editor and Founder of *Craft International*, writes for *Art in America* and *Arts* magazines and the *East Hampton Star*. She is at work on her first book of poems.

Roger Skillings has been associated with the Fine Arts Work Center since 1969 and has published three books of stories: *Alternative Lives*, *P-town Stories* and *In A Murderous Time*.

Tom Sleigh, a former Fine Arts Work Center fellow, has published a collection of poems entitled *After One* (Houghton Mifflin, 1983).

Bruce Smith was a Fine Arts Work Center fellow. His most recent book of poems, *Silver and Information* (University of Georgia Press, 1985), appeared in the National Poetry Series.

William Jay Smith has recently published *Collected Translations: Italian, French, Spanish, Portuguese* (New Rivers) and a translation of *Moral Tales* by Jules Laforgue (New Directions). He is currently preparing a volume of his collected poems.

William Stafford's most recent collection is entitled *Smoke's Ways: Poems from Limited Editions* (Graywolf, 1983).

May **Swenson's** latest book of poetry is *New and Selected Things Taking Place* (Little, Brown, 1978).

Tomas Tranströmer, the well-known Swedish poet, has been translated by Robert Bly and May Swenson.

Ellen Bryant Voigt's most recent collection of poetry is *The Forces of Plenty* (Norton, 1983).

Richard Wilbur's sixth book, *Opposites: Poems and Drawings,* was published by Harcourt Brace Jovanovich in 1979.

C. K. Williams most recently published *Tar* (Random House, 1983).

Charles Wright's fifth book, *Country Music,* was published by Random House in 1982.